HOW TO USE
THE POWER OF MIND
in everyday life

How to use the POWER of MIND

in everyday life

CRAIG CARTER

Science of Mind Publications
Los Angeles, California

First Printing — October 1976

Published by SCIENCE OF MIND PUBLICATIONS
3251 West Sixth Street—P.O. Box 75127
Los Angeles, California 90075
Copyright © 1976 by Science of Mind Publications
All Rights Reserved
Printed in the United States of America
ISBN 0-911336-65-6

Cover illustration: Norman Merritt

CONTENTS

SECTION ONE

*Basic Principles and Methods of the Science of Mind
for Dealing with Human Problems in General*

SECTION TWO

*Methods of Treatment in the Science of Mind
for Various Human Problems of a Specific Nature*

SECTION THREE

Using the Science of Mind for Answering Questions
Most Often Asked in Spiritual Counseling Situations

FOREWORD

This is a book of remarkable power. A glance at the table of contents gives an idea of its unusual scope, while inspection of any individual page will reveal the confidence with which it approaches human problems. From God and Miracles to Teenagers and Having Enough Money, it addresses itself to an impressive range of circumstances and questions.

But, whole libraries already overflow with volumes written about God; vendors peddle scores of books on prosperity; essays on improving relationships and helping your children are found by the hundreds every month on newsstands. What can this book possibly add?

The secret of *How To Use The Power Of Mind* is that instead of suggesting a vast number of solutions to life's challenges, it offers a single, simple *method* by which anyone, at any level of understanding, may probe directly into the Source of Life, a place of Infinite Potential, emerging with answers that are precisely individualized in terms of any question which might be asked. Learn the principle of addition and subtraction, and you may perform endless arithmetic operations. Likewise, learn the principles of finding answers to life's dilemmas, and you might as well have discovered a wonderful kind of magic.

This book talks in terms of that Source and those principles, giving numerous and varied suggestions as to *specifically how* they may be used. Thus, this is much more than simply an assortment of nice ideas, for it is, as its title explicitly states, a "how-to" manual.

It is based on the teachings of Dr. Ernest Holmes (1887–1960) and his classic metaphysical textbook, *The Science of Mind* (Dodd, Mead & Co., 1938). That book and the philosophy it explains were the product of Dr. Holmes' extensive study of the world's great spiritual systems and his synthesis of the ideas which all of those systems share. His synthesis—simple, comprehensive, and devoid of dogma—was what he described as "a result of the best thought of the ages." It was not, he stressed, his personal opinion nor was it a special revelation.

It did, however, contain his great contribution to modern spiritual thought: a *method* by which the principles of Life Itself could be used. It is this method which is at the core of *How To Use The Power Of Mind* and which is explained so lucidly by Dr. Craig Carter, a long-time personal student of Dr. Holmes, and widely known as a teacher of the Science of Mind philosophy.

To deal with the essential principles of existence is to deal with invisible things. No one has seen the principle of arithmetic, yet no one doubts that it exists. It is what makes arithmetic work; it is why two

1

plus two always gives four. Similarly, no one has seen the principles of Life, Truth, or Love, though all who live, seek truth, or know love do not doubt their existence. The universe, in fact, is abundant with basic principles, yet because they are invisible, mankind has given to their functioning an array of mysterious interpretations, often presuming that their operation might be understood only by the fortunately born or the specially initiated. From these various interpretations, mankind has derived all religions. But if the many different and often conflicting dogmas are confusing, Principle is not and never has been. It is simply the activity of Life, of Existence, of the Source which created all things—ourselves included. And that Source is Love. It is ultimate Energy. It is all of our highest values extended beyond our ability to know them as being high. It is what some call God. Ernest Holmes, desiring to distinguish ideas about It from the unclear pre-conceptions of many people, often called It simply, "The Thing Itself."

To learn how to align oneself with this Source is to learn how to live constructively; to be happy, healthy, prosperous, straight-headed, and secure. That is what the material in these pages tells how to do.

Particularly today, with so many people aware of a transcendent universe, thinking in terms of karma and of life's unseen dimensions, there is a tendency to feel trapped, victimized by unknowable forces. This book and the methods of the Science of Mind show why and how anyone, at any time, may claim freedom in a spiritual universe.

—Science of Mind Publications

(The material in this book originally appeared, in slightly different form, in various issues of Science of Mind *Magazine. Brought together here for the first time, it has been specially revised by the author, who has written three introductory essays for this edition.)*

SECTION ONE

Basic Principles and Methods of the
Science of Mind
for Dealing with Human Problems in General

INTRODUCTION—I

There must be very few people who have not discovered that when things go wrong and you say something wrong to go with them, they don't tend to get any better.

When things go wrong, say something right!

There is your basic rule for using the Science of Mind to meet and overcome—to "heal"—human problems. "Turn from the problem to the answer, and say the answer out loud!" This book tells you how to do it.

Is that formula an over-simplification? Of course it is. There is much more involved in the field of spiritual healing, but no matter how complex may be the system of meditation, treatment, or prayer; or by whatever school of religion, philosophy, psychology, or psychosomatic medicine it may be devised, the fact remains that all healing by spiritual means follows upon a state of consciousness which identifies with *answers* and denies problems. If, for example, your consciousness is one of sickness, you will be sick. Deliberately alter it to one of well-being (prosperity, love, security, happiness, or whatever good thing you desire), and you will soon have that which corresponds to the new state of your belief.

This happens because behind every condition is a belief, and if you can change the belief, you can change the condition. There will, again, be those who ask, "Isn't this also too simplistic?" But now the response is different, for while the implications of this cause-effect relationship may be extremely complex in application, the Principle *is* simplicity itself! If you, the Seeker, will go to the Ages, to the philosophers, to the psychoanalysts, to any of the schools of New Thought, or even to the scriptures of Christianity, you will find that this, in essence, is what all have said: *it is done unto you according to your belief!* And the changing of your belief is entirely within your own control.

Because the outer world of your personal experience follows the model of your inner world of mental causation, every time you say, "I am . . ." and add something to it, you set into motion a mental Law of Correspondence, which tends to bring about in actual experience whatever corresponds to your word—your state of consciousness—about yourself. Say, "I feel wonderful!" and that Law will bring you more of something to feel wonderful about. But say to yourself, "I am tired," and you most certainly will be.

Then one day you may encounter a friend who asks, "Do you suppose you are tired all the time because you are doing work not meant for you? That you therefore oppose it subconsciously and arise from your nightly sleep *already weary* at the day's prospects?"

If this friend knew you can change your experience by changing your mental state, he might suggest that you begin a discipline of definite mental activity in which you affirm: "I know that somewhere in this world there is work exactly right for me to do. I shall not be satisfied until I find it. I affirm that a Universal Wisdom is revealing it to me right now . . . that I am guided in right directions, to right people, at right times. Gratefully, I know I am now moving into my right place in life!"

What a powerful statement that is! How different from "agreeing" with tiredness. What a dramatic change of consciousness it embodies, as it turns boldly from the problem and fixes with absolute certainty on the answer. And this is precisely the sort of "consciousness change" which must be incorporated into the thinking of anyone who would use the Science of Mind to heal problems.

Throughout this book, you will find example after example of just such healing thoughts, those which open the way to a changed state of consciousness. They are statements you may make about yourself, the sorts of "spiritual mind treatments" you can give. These treatments will work both for the healing of specific things that are wrong in your life, and also, in a general sense, for the unfoldment of your very soul along paths of spiritual righteousness and accomplishment.

In this first section, you will find a clear, step-by-step explanation of the theory of the Science of Mind (in light type), followed by specific examples for practice (in boldface type). It is these examples which you should speak aloud.

Almost immediately, you will encounter some statement such as, "I am at peace," and you will respond, "Well, that certainly isn't true about *me*!" But remember that you are now turning to answers, and your task is to convince yourself that what you want to be true *is* true in the realm of Divine Perfection. If you are able instantly to embody an awareness of perfect peace, that is fine. But if you cannot achieve such an immediate realization, you must anticipate "arguing" with yourself. This is a standard technique by which you affirm your belief in peace, denying any contrary appearance, disputing the reality of problems, asserting your belief in answers. Continuing in this fashion, your goal is to attain that state of realization where you can say, *believing,* "I am at peace." And at that moment, the great Law of Life will, in truth, have brought you peace!

With the lessons which follow, guide yourself to answers and begin that most rewarding of all adventures: taking charge of your life by creating your own destiny!

REVERSING "NEGATIVE" THOUGHT

The simplest form of treatment is to "reverse the thought." This means that when a thought of lack comes to mind we should instantly say mentally, "There is no lack in the kingdom of God, and I am right there, right now!"

It is said that anything we think, say, or do three times establishes a habit groove in the nervous system. We are the victims of our bad habits. *But we are also the beneficiaries of our good habits!* We cannot function outside of natural laws and habit patterns, but we can very definitely build new response patterns into our body, our personality, our prayer life.

The reversing of a negative thought is the only intelligent thing to do with it. Nothing is gained if a salesman who has had a run of unfruitful calls says to himself, "I'm a failure. I can't make it. I'll lose my car. What has Smith got that I haven't got?" These are seed thoughts of failure and will grow as easily as the ones of success. He should reverse these thoughts and think, "Well, I missed a couple! So what? I know my product is good. I know I can sell it. I can sell anything. I'm on my way to the contacts that result in good business."

And he is, too! This is valid "treatment" and it will work. This method can be applied to any type of negative thinking. Try it out today! All day!

Treatment for Positive Patterns

This is the day I keep my thoughts positive and hopeful. Every time I have a negative reaction, I will reverse it with a positive statement of faith. Today is a new beginning, and I have faith that it brings me every kind of good. I accept this as true.

Be ye reformed in the newness of your wit.
—Romans 12:2 (fifteenth-century translation)

WE MUST CONCEIVE OF THE SPIRIT, GOD, AS GOVERNING, CONTROLLING AND DIRECTING MAN'S ACTIVITY. GOD IS NOT A FAILURE. THEREFORE, WE MUST RESOLUTELY TURN AWAY FROM EVERY EXPERIENCE WHICH HAS BEEN NEGATIVE. . . .
—*The Science of Mind,* page 315

GOD IS ONE—GOD IS ALL

Before we go further into methods of treatment, let us reflect upon the glorious *Presence* that is the source of our being, whose Wisdom is infinite, whose Action empowers us and all of our good!

This One that is God, is the "Beloved One" of the ages, the heart and life of poet, mystic, lover. This One is the Self-Existent. Clothed in human imagery, It is the *Mother* of the Hindu, the *Father* of the Jew, the *Christ* of the West, and the *Buddha* of the East. Yet, It is always and ever One!

"Be still, and know that I am God . . . ."

God sings in the poet, laughs in the child, moves with the dancer, and captures His own beauty with the artist's brush.

This is mysticism. It is the one unchanging vision. No mystic in any age has seen that which confutes another's seeing. Dogmas change and ethics alter; customs decay and opinions are born; but *that One* is constant. And man *is* one with this undivided One. We should capture this vision and have all faith in it, for in it we shall find our freedom and our power. And in truth as we *do* understand these more mystical ideas, we *are* "giving a treatment," because as Dr. Holmes wrote: "We treat with our understanding."

Treatment for God-Awareness

I enter now into a silent recognition of the Presence of God. The spirit of the almighty One is around and about me, and is the life within me. It is that which I am. I am still. I am at peace. I am aware of the Presence of God.

Now unto the King eternal, immortal, invisible, the only wise God, be honour and glory for ever and ever. Amen. I Timothy 1:17

ALL MEN SEEK SOME RELATIONSHIP TO THE UNIVERSAL MIND, THE OVER-SOUL, OR THE ETERNAL SPIRIT, WHICH WE CALL GOD. AND LIFE REVEALS ITSELF TO WHOEVER IS RECEPTIVE TO IT.

—*The Science of Mind*, page 32

INSTANTANEOUS TREATMENT

In addition to "reversing the thought," another very simple form of *treatment* is one where we shift our attention from the problem to the answer—somewhat as a modern automobile transmission automatically shifts to a higher gear as the car picks up speed.

It works like this: When you find yourself worrying about something, feeling tense, or faced with a problem, stop for a moment right in the middle of your mental muddle and *remember God!* Let your awareness suddenly shift to remembering that God is with you, that God is the answer, that with God all things are possible.

You know what it is like to have your attention suddenly captured by a sound, a light, or a startling scenic view. You forget everything else for a moment. Let it be like this when, in the midst of looking at your problem, you suddenly *remember God,* and that God can help you—so you just stop right there, and you don't even think, or make affirmations of faith, but you just silently "look toward God," from whom is all your strength!

At first, the mind is undisciplined and slips right back to the problem, or starts telling God what to do about it, or starts telling you it can't be done! But with practice, you learn to be still as your awareness stays for a little while in the God-Presence, in a silent knowing that God is All.

Treatment for Instant Help

God is here. God is now. God is my life. God is the answer. I accept help now. I give thanks for God's help right now! I believe in God and in His infinite Wisdom and my mind is quiet now as I silently accept His action making all things right in this situation.

For the word of God is quick, and powerful, and sharper than any two-edged sword. . . . —Hebrews 4:12

THE BIRTH OF THE SOUL INTO THE LIGHT OF SPIRIT IS AN AWAKENING TO THE REALIZATION THAT GOD HAS BEEN WITH US ALL THE TIME. "NOW ARE WE THE SONS OF GOD."

—*The Science of Mind,* page 503

9

RELATIONSHIP OF MAN TO GOD

Whatever form of treatment is used, from the simple methods so far described to the more complex ones to follow, there is always involved a basic response of Spirit: *From the heart of man a cry; from the heart of God, reply!*

In more direct language, there is always that within us which yearns, desires, seeks—and it always yearns *for* something. Even if one achieves a complete awareness of unity, and one should expect to do exactly that, it took an *initial intention* to bring this about, and that intention had to be as personal as the heartbeat of the man who had it! So the *person* is most definitely involved.

Yet, of ourselves we are nothing! Except a man leave his lesser self, he cannot gain his greater self. That for which we yearn and to which we turn, is greater than we are. We approach It "with awe, but not with fear." And the great and wise have said that God responds to man to the extent that man recognizes God.

So this is the great emergent vision: Man shall initiate a consciousness of God, which will lift him to the awareness of "perfect Spirit, perfectly present." Thus *to practice the Presence of God* is to become consciously One with God. Essentially, this is what every treatment should accomplish, whatever the treatment method we employ.

Treatment for Personal Affairs

Today I know that *perfect Spirit, perfectly present,* **is my fulfillment. There is only One God, whose Life and Power flows through my life now. I trust my affairs to the wise guidance and loving action of the Spirit Divine.**

And, behold, I am with thee, and will keep thee in all places whither thou goest. . . . —Genesis 28:15

THE TEACHING OF THE MYSTICS HAS BEEN THAT THERE SHOULD BE *conscious courting of the Divine Presence.* THERE SHOULD BE A CONSCIOUS RECEPTIVITY TO IT, *but a balanced one.*
—*The Science of Mind,* page 329

TWO BASIC ELEMENTS IN TREATMENT

The two basic elements in treatment could be summed up in the terms: *unify* and *specify*.

A treatment which starts with a sick man will end with a sick man. We must start with God, who is never sick, and whose Spirit in man is also not subject to illness. Therefore, we first *unify* our thought with God, in whatever manner is natural to us as individuals. If we see God as Love, then let us endeavor in prayer or contemplation to feel our unity with that Love, and to know that we are some part of It, and that It is personal to us.

Then, and very clearly—as clearly as we can—let us see this Love as a healing power, and *specify* our acceptance of the healing needed in our particular case. If we have a specific problem, we now let our acceptance of the solution become specific at the point of that problem. We know that Love can meet every human need, and that our consciousness of It meets our particular need now. So we return to an awareness of Love, of God, of perfect Spirit, perfectly present. We sense our unity with this Spiritual Presence, dropping our concern over the problem, and seeing only our total immersion in Its healing action. We have faith that Divine Love knows how to fulfill our need.

Treatment for General Health

I believe in God. I believe that God's Spirit and His Substance is the Source of all form. My body is formed of Divine Substance, and is therefore part of God's Perfection and Love. I contemplate this Perfection and declare that It is made visible in me now.

Call unto me, and I will answer thee, and shew thee great and mighty things, which thou knowest not. —Jeremiah 33:3

THE GREATEST GOOD THAT CAN COME TO ANYONE IS THE FORMING WITHIN HIM OF AN ABSOLUTE CERTAINTY OF HIMSELF, AND OF HIS RELATIONSHIP TO THE UNIVERSE, FOREVER REMOVING THE SENSE OF HEAVEN AS BEING OUTSIDE HIMSELF.

—*The Science of Mind,* page 180

GIVE DIRECTION TO YOUR THOUGHTS

Let us emphasize a point that many are a long time learning; namely, that "treatment" is something that must be *done,* and is not done until you *do* it! Thoughts and aspirations must be cleared of negation, doubt, fear, and pin-pointed constructively. Your *undefined* desire remains but a longing hope, changing nothing in your experience. Therefore, we emphasize this rule: Give voice to your conviction that the God within you responds to your thoughts through corresponding to the images of your perception and conviction.

The various methods of treatment will in time become second nature. The thing to do, right now, is to start *voicing your thoughts* to yourself and to the God within you.

Those who are haphazard about doing this wonder why they do not get the results others do. Some read this philosophy, but say, "It does not seem to work for me, although I know it is logically right." They have not realized that they, personally, must not only take time to analyze and direct their thinking, but must also give personal voice to their healing thoughts.

Give voice to your thoughts. Is God Love? Say so. "God is Love." Where do you think God is? Do you believe God is everywhere and thus right where you are? Say so. Say what you think, what you believe. If what you believe is equivalent to what is *true,* your saying it aloud will *personalize* that truth *for you,* in your affairs, in your health, and in your relationships.

Treatment for Relationships

I now accept God's Love as the law of all my relationships with other people. I see God's Life in them; their life in God. I am in harmony with that Life, for it is my life, too. The God in me salutes the God in all whom I meet today. For this blessing I do give thanks.

I will sing of the mercies of the Lord for ever: with my mouth will I make known thy faithfulness to all generations. —Psalm 89:1

THE WORD WHICH CARRIES POWER IS THE ONE WHICH HAS CONVICTION BACK OF IT. —*The Science of Mind,* page 176

ARGUMENTATION AND REALIZATION

Having emphasized previously the need for actually *speaking* our word for healing, we now consider another side of the picture —that of *silence* and its place in our healing practice.

Its place is very great, indeed. One moment of *silent realization* is worth all the spoken words! Why, then, do we use words at all? To bring us *to* that moment of realization. Because unless we can at least approximate in word-images that which we seek to realize, the realization has no model to follow. Realization is simply the fruit of recognition.

When you realize peace, you will *be* at peace. It will be such peace as you have described and embodied. If, however, you are still anxious, or if you have merely achieved a certain *resignation,* then real peace is not yet in you, and you should return to your speaking of *words which have peace in them* until at last you can be still, and let that peace which passes understanding become your experience in the silence.

When you do have such an experience, you see why *realization* is greater than *argumentation.* Yet remember that each of these is an element in the building of a healing consciousness. We use *argumentation* to bring our awareness to the point of *realization.* And even if, through practice, one learns to achieve *instant realization,* behind this will lie all the words of conviction one has ever uttered in argumentation.

Treatment for Peace

I contemplate now the goodness, the right action, and the nearness of God, who is within me. I am immersed in Beauty and Truth. I am *in tune with the Infinite*. I know that Peace is the power at the heart of God. In God I live and move and have my being. His Peace is the power at the center of me!

. . . there is a spirit in man: and the inspiration of the Almighty giveth them understanding.   —Job 32:8

ALL EMERGE FROM THAT ONE WHOSE BEING IS EVER PRESENT AND WHOSE LIFE, ROBED IN NUMBERLESS FORMS, IS MANIFEST THROUGH-OUT ALL CREATION.   —*The Science of Mind,* page 420

WHY TREATMENT SOMETIMES FAILS

When a treatment fails to produce the desired result, we have to remember that it wasn't the Law by which it operates that failed. It was the person using the Law. And the most common mistake we make, probably, is to neutralize our words of faith by words of failure!

One thing people often find difficult to demonstrate is a greater material prosperity. They make fine affirmations, such as "Money is God in action," and then complain about the prices these days, and the income tax, and that "some guys are lucky. Look at that house of his!"

Well, there is no such thing as luck; and until you heal yourself of envy, you won't be having the money for a better house. Until you are grateful for the income you pay your tax on you are in danger of losing it altogether. If prices are high, the income will be too for those who stop saying unpleasant things about money and start blessing every dollar that passes through their hands.

If you believe that it is right and good to be prosperous, then give yourself treatments for the acceptance of your total good, and include the material things of life because they are good. And watch what you say *outside* of your treatment period, for it is there that your beliefs are revealed, too.

It is done unto us as we *really* believe, not just as we *say* we believe!

Treatment for Prosperity

I am grateful for everything I have. I enjoy my possessions, but I am not possessed by them. I enjoy prosperity, and I am glad to spend as freely as I receive! I share what I have, and I always have more than enough to share. For its right and good use, I bless all that I have, all that I receive, all that I give.

But let him ask in faith, nothing wavering. For he that wavereth is like a wave of the sea driven with the wind and tossed. —James 1:6

THE REASON THAT WE DO NOT DEMONSTRATE MORE EASILY IS THAT THE SUBJECTIVE STATE OF OUR THOUGHT IS TOO OFTEN NEUTRALIZED BY THE OBJECTIVE STATE, THOUGH OFTEN THIS IS AN UNCONSCIOUS PROCESS OF THOUGHT. —*The Science of Mind*, page 119

THREE-STAGE METHOD OF TREATMENT

One method of treatment embodies three steps which we may designate as recognition, unification, and command. We mean by these terms: RECOGNITION of the Presence and the Power of God, awareness of our UNIFICATION with that same Presence, and the COMMAND of our word in keeping with God's Wisdom.

In still more detail, we endeavor in the first stage to understand that the Spirit in man is the God-Presence, which is infinite and loving. Man's thought is a channel through which It creates and that creativity is brought forth through what we term *Law*, unlimited, impersonal, and infallible in expressing the ideas given It. In the second stage we make our identification (unification) with this personalness of God. And finally, we move in our mental action to a specific application, to *command*, as we speak our word for the fulfillment of our need.

The textbook, *The Science of Mind*, explains this in terms of the story of Jesus at Lazarus' tomb. "Father, I thank thee that thou hast heard me," is the recognition of the Presence of God; "I knew that thou hearest me always," is the conviction of unification with that Presence; "Lazarus, come forth," is the word of authority spoken out of that conviction.

We have the privilege of directing our own thinking; when we let it be in harmony with the Power greater than we are, we bring our experiences out of the tomb of limitation.

Treatment to Remove False Conditions

I know that there is no power opposed to God. There is no false growth or wrong condition in God's Life. That Life is my life now. I let go of every contrary belief. I believe only in God, and I give myself utterly to His right action in my life.

. . . And Jesus lifted up his eyes, and said, Father, I thank thee that thou hast heard me. —John 11:41

FIRST, REALIZE THAT DIVINE POWER IS; THEN UNIFY WITH IT; AND THEN SPEAK THE WORD AS "ONE HAVING AUTHORITY," FOR THE LAW IS "THE SERVANT OF THE ETERNAL SPIRIT THROUGHOUT ALL THE AGES." —*The Science of Mind*, page 332

RECOGNITION OF GOD'S PRESENCE AND POWER

By some inner process of consciousness, vocalized or sensed, one becomes aware that there is a spiritual Presence—an infinite Spirit, God, or Divine Intelligence. We learn to know the nearness, the goodness, and the allness of God.

Upon suddenly having a new idea, we sometimes recognize this as something we already knew, but had not remembered or had not fully realized. Something awakens us as we pray or meditate, and we know with a new conviction that which we have already believed.

Perhaps, the most necessary phase of our particular work is that of *acceptance*. You and I should give our fullest recognition, in this sense, to the fact that the laws of God are always just and good, and that from God alone is all authority and power. We need to see, sense, and accept the Perfection of God in and throughout the universe, in and throughout our world, and in and throughout our own personal being—our mind, body, and affairs.

Treatment for Happiness

God's child is happy, and I am God's child! This is a good world, full of good people who are my friends, and replete with things, places, and events that are enjoyable. I recognize God's Presence and I accept my right place in a happy, God-created world! Under His guidance I shall not be greatly moved into accepting other than that which is of His nature.

———————

Truly my soul waiteth upon God: from him cometh my salvation. He only is my rock and my salvation; he is my defence; I shall not be greatly moved. —Psalm 62:1-2

MAN IS IN GOD AND GOD IS MAN, JUST AS A DROP OF WATER IS IN THE OCEAN, WHILE THE OCEAN IS THE DROP OF WATER. THIS IS THE RECOGNITION WHICH JESUS HAD WHEN HE SAID, "I AND THE FATHER ARE ONE." —*The Science of Mind,* page 331

GOD IS LIFE—OUR LIFE IS GOD

When we move in our consciousness from a *silent recognition* of the God-Presence and God-Power to a *conscious unification* with that Presence, then we should speak forth our faith. This is the place in our *positive prayer* where we identify our own life with God-Life, our own mind with Divine Mind.

There can be only One Mind—and our mind is part of It. We often limit the idea of Mind in terms of our own thinking, which is, indeed, personal and largely limited to the vocabulary and capacity of the thinker; but the principle of Mind itself is unlimited and universal, and goes infinitely beyond our personal understanding. In treatment we lay claim upon the perfect knowledge and action of this greater Mind, and we know that the answer to our need can and does manifest as a result of our personal faith, and in terms personal to our need.

God is Life. Our living is an embodiment of that Life. At this point in our treatment we must very clearly acknowledge our individual embodiment of this perfect Life. There can be no question here. It is impossible that we could live apart from Life Itself. Our proclaiming this brings us to a conscious unification with the healing Presence. And all the qualities of that Presence indwell Its manifestation in ourselves, and in those others for whom we may also be treating.

Treatment for Healing

Infinite Mind knows only good, and is not confused. I let that Mind be wholly expressed in me. I now see the Father's Perfection in all that I am. It knows how to heal me, and I release my needs to God's action and see myself whole and perfect.

I have said, Ye are gods; and all of you are children of the most High.
—Psalm 82:6

WE RECOGNIZE, THEN, IN MAN'S SELF-KNOWING MIND HIS UNITY WITH THE WHOLE; FOR WHILE A DROP OF WATER IS NOT THE OCEAN, YET IT DOES CONTAIN WITHIN ITSELF ALL THE ATTRIBUTES OF THE LIMITLESS DEEP. —*The Science of Mind*, page 121

CONSCIOUS DIRECTION OF SPIRITUAL LAW

Love is only a potential until someone is loved. There is no knowledge outside of something known. Consciousness must be conscious of something. All such statements imply that it is futile to postulate a truth apart from the way it works. It is futile to think that any idea can be beyond the Law of Cause and Effect. Every thought we think is itself a causation and must have some effect in our lives.

We think of God as Divine Causation, the Self-Existent Perfection, and of man as some part of the Divine Life. But few of us have awakened to the completeness of ourselves in God, and through the God-given ability of choice we often choose ideas that could never result in our good. However, we can rise in consciousness from the level of the ideas that produced a problem to the level of those ideas that can solve it.

The third step in the three-step treatment method—*command* —will be understood only when we accept, once and for all, that we have the ability consciously to direct our own thinking and thereby to use the great Law of Mind for our betterment. In a treatment, the recognition and unification of our thought with God's Good brings us to the point of specific use. Whatever we then embody in our thought constitutes a demand upon the Law to create it in our experience.

Treatment to Overcome Doubt

I am now going to be so still that the silence speaks to me of God. It tells me: "Be still, and know that I am God." I cannot doubt as I take dominion over my own thinking. God is my Strength and my Redeemer. I let this day bear witness to His activity through me in every avenue of my life, and in specific terms of mind, body, and affairs.

Thou madest him to have dominion over the works of thy hands: thou has put all things under his feet. —Psalm 8:6

A PRACTITIONER, THEN, IS ONE WHO, RECOGNIZING THE POWER OF MIND, DEFINITELY, SPECIFICALLY, CONCRETELY, AND CONSCIOUSLY . . . GIVES DIRECTION TO A LAW, WHICH IS THE ACTOR.

—*The Science of Mind,* page 169

TYPES OF "COMMAND" IN TREATMENT

We should accept the idea that in treatment for healing a definite situation, there must be an element of specific intention. Let us consider some of the forms this may take.

It may take the form of actual command. We have a right to say to inharmony, "Begone! I no longer accept you!" Or perhaps this strong statement of denial, "There is no inharmony in God. There is no inharmony between me and any other person of God's creation!" Or we may affirm, "All inharmonious conditions are now dissolved as I accept only God's right action through my affairs."

We may prefer not to consider the details of our problem once we begin treatment. We may find we work best by losing ourselves in the consciousness of the good we desire to achieve, rather than to dwell overmuch upon the thing we wish to be rid of. Or we may actually say, "The intention of this treatment is that inharmony shall be removed from my relationship with (name the person)," and then forget whatever is *wrong,* and become conscious of all that is *right,* by recognition of the Presence of God in the midst of each, and by personal unification with that Presence.

Treatment to Eliminate Discord

I now turn to the Presence within me and acknowledge Its action in this situation confronting me. God's Love sustains me as well as the other person, guiding us into perfect harmony and peace. There is no obstacle It cannot surmount, and I let It banish all discord from this experience, right now!

Blessed are they that keep his testimonies, and that seek him with the whole heart. —Psalm 119:2

THE WORD WHICH CARRIES POWER IS THE ONE WHICH HAS CONVICTION BACK OF IT. LET US NOT BLITHELY REPEAT WORDS. . . .
—*The Science of Mind,* page 176

WORKING FOR RIGHT ACTION

A good time to use the three-step treatment method is when the solution of a problem defies our imagination, or its cause escapes our analysis. There are circumstances where we cannot see just what went wrong. We do not understand it, or there would be no problem. In this case we treat for what we call "right action."

We know, first, that with God all things are possible. Therefore, *whatever* this problem is, there *is* a right answer to it. We then acknowledge our willingness to be healed of whatever is in ourselves that brought this situation about. We try to realize that regardless of appearances, the Spirit of God is everywhere present, and is present in all who may be involved in our problem. This Presence is the Source of "righteous judgment," and we seek to recognize only God's Wisdom as guiding and directing all concerned.

Finally, we bring into our meditation a definite element of expectation. We really do expect "right action" to take place. We say so. We affirm our faith in it. We give thanks, and release the treatment, knowing that our word cannot return to us void!

Treatment for Right Action

I know that Divine Mind can meet every human need. I am One with the Father, and nothing stands in the way of my faith and my willingness to accept His right action, now, in this problem that concerns me.

Commit thy way unto the Lord; trust also in him; and he shall bring it to pass. —Psalm 37:5

MAN IS A CENTER OF GOD-CONSCIOUSNESS IN THE GREAT WHOLE. . . . TURNING TO THE ONE WITH A COMPLETE ABANDONMENT AND IN ABSOLUTE TRUST, HE WILL FIND THAT HE IS ALREADY SAVED, HEALED, AND PROSPERED. —*The Science of Mind,* page 323

THE SIX FACTORS IN TREATMENT

Let us now take a new approach, for some of the basic factors in spiritual mind treatment may best be described as steps in a technique, or method, somewhat more comprehensive than those we have so far considered.

There are six key words in a model treatment outline, and they will be taken up one at a time in these lessons.

The key words are: *God, Self, Intention, Denial, Affirmations* and *Release.*

Spiritual mind treatment consists in taking each of these ideas, one by one, and staying with it until there is a sense of full awareness and completion in our own inner conviction. Treatment begins and ends with a consciousness of God. Forgetting all else, one begins speaking, or mentally contemplating, the things one *believes* about Deity, the transcendent, the all-powerful, the infinite One. This is part of the *recognition* phase of our work as described previously. But if a healing from this earlier work has not been manifested, let us now be willing to re-examine the *way* we have been working. Do we have a really clear concept of God, and *can we put it into real words?* Perhaps we are expecting definite results from an indefinite set of beliefs. Unfortunately, this doesn't work! Vague consciousness gets vague results only. We should have the fire of real spiritual conviction. We should know that *all there really is, is God,* and we should say so.

Treatment for Inner Conviction

With all my heart I am convinced that God is all, in all. The manifest universe is the Body of God. Our life is the Spirit of God in us. All of our power is from God, and God is everywhere wholly present.

Blessed is the man that trusteth in the Lord, and whose hope the Lord is.   —Jeremiah 17:7

TO RISE ABOVE THE CONTEMPLATION OF CONDITIONS IS TO ENTER THAT FIELD OF CAUSATION WHICH MAKES ALL THINGS NEW IN OUR EXPERIENCE.   —*The Science of Mind,* page 414

THE PERSONALNESS OF GOD

There is a need for peace of mind in regard to recognizing and accepting the Divinity of our own individual being. If the quality of *personalness* were not part of the nature of God, no individual expressions of His Life could ever have appeared, for God is the only Creator. But Life *does* manifest in us. Life *is* in you and in me, and we *are* here, and we cannot explain ourselves away as some part of a cosmic delusion or a material accident.

As we have contemplated Divine Reality as the first step of our new treatment method, we will now contemplate that same Reality as the only Source of our own personal being. It is in the life that God has given us that we will find our Divinity!

Let us pronounce aloud our belief that, "There is One Life, that Life is God, that Life is perfect, and that Life is my life now!" This statement has great healing power as an affirmation of faith. Together with the development of each of the other ideas in our "six-step-method," this step of *unification* with our Creator will bring our consciousness to a realization that heals. We know that "we, of ourselves, do nothing," but we do recognize the Father within, for "he doeth the works."

Something in your heart must accept, and must not reject, your Oneness with the Father. Somewhere, false humility must end if real identification is to begin.

Treatment for Self-Realization

In me is life, and that life is of God. And in me is love, for the Father's Love alone brings forth the Son. I believe in the Christ-Spirit—the Son of the living God within me. That which God is, is born in man, as man.

The spirit of God hath made me, and the breath of the Almighty hath given me life.   —Job 33:4

TO CONTEMPLATE THAT DIVINE LIFE WHICH IS AT THE VERY CENTER OF EVERYMAN'S LIFE—THIS IS THE VERY ESSENCE OF MENTAL HEALING.
                                        —*The Science of Mind,* page 409

THE IMPORTANCE OF CLEAR EXPECTATION

There is certainly such a thing as the prayer which seeks only to express love, reverence, and gratitude. It is perhaps the highest form of prayer. And very probably, if we practiced this kind of prayer-life, no problems would ever arise in our living.

So when a problem *does* arise in our living, we may be sure that somewhere we have failed to cooperate with the Perfection of the Spirit within us in regard to the laws of Its function. We have failed to recognize or accept It, and the "flow" of perfect expression within us has been interrupted. The purpose of treatment is to bring *ourselves*—not God—back to perfect expression. It is our thoughts and beliefs that must be healed—and they must *be* healed if our problem is to be solved.

This kind of prayer, then, does have purpose—and the purpose is admittedly specific. It is good to enter into the gates of the Lord with thanksgiving and make known our need for understanding and help.

Therefore an essential step in treatment is knowing that our need, our good desire, is being met. We must expect the healing of the problem we are treating for. *We should clearly state this expectation.* The inner self, we repeat, is not convinced by a shallow thought, or one we are unable or unwilling to put into honest language!

Treatment for Clear Expression

I believe that Divine Intelligence is the heritage of man, and the Source of my own understanding. I release this word as a thought-seed planted in Mind, and I know that I daily find myself improving in self-expression; clearly, honestly, and with ease.

As for me, I will call upon God; and the Lord shall save me.

—Psalm 55:16

A PRACTITIONER USES THOUGHT DEFINITELY AND FOR SPECIFIC PURPOSES, AND THE MORE DEFINITELY HE USES THE LAW, THE MORE DIRECTLY WILL IT RESPOND TO HIM.

—*The Science of Mind,* page 54

THE PLACE OF DENIALS IN TREATMENT

The fourth step in our structure of a complete and detailed spiritual mind treatment is to deny or neutralize any idea that there is a Divine necessity for whatever negative appearances may present themselves in the problem being treated. These negative factors may be inherent in the situation itself, or they may be unhappy or fearful thoughts or emotions in our own consciousness.

We have already explained how treatment, as a process, is intended to correct the wrong *beliefs* of the person or persons involved in a troublesome situation; and it is not unusual to find beliefs of fear, doubt, or discouragement still in our own heart, even as we are trying our best to give a good treatment.

The thing to do is *to deny all such negative thoughts and feelings,* with clear and forceful statements. You will feel yourself suddenly comforted with a realization that what you have been saying is true: there really *is no fear* in the heart of God, and no pain. God's Peace is never disturbed or shaken. If you say these things knowing that God's nature indwells you and this is what you *want to accept,* then it will be so.

There is power in honesty, in "facing up to things." Do not skip this "denial" step in spiritual mind treatment because of some sort of suspicion that denial should have no place in a treatment. On the contrary, the right kind of denial is a form of affirmation.

Treatment to Overcome Fears

I am completely secure and safe in the kingdom of God, right where I am. No appearance, no thought, no mystery can disturb me. There is no power opposed to God. The perfect Love of God within me casteth out all fear!

What time I am afraid, I will trust in thee. —Psalm 56:3

THE PRACTITIONER MUST KNOW, AND MUST STATE, THAT THERE ARE NO OBSTACLES IN THE PATHWAY OF TRUTH. —*The Science of Mind,* page 59

THE IMPORTANCE OF AFFIRMATIONS

We come now to the affirmation of our faith, to the announcement and pronouncement of our good.

This is a wonderful part of spiritual mind treatment, for by now we should have an awareness of the nature of God and our relationship to Him. We have recognized God as the Spirit within us and have accepted the intention of our treatment as directed to our need. We have firmly laid aside all that would in any way obstruct or interrupt our perfect realization of a completed manifestation.

Now we must begin to affirm that manifestation. We will come to know how it is that at a certain point it seems as though the Spirit Itself had taken over the treatment! We are still completely ourselves, of course, but yet we seem now to be more than ourselves. And we are! We find ourselves at this latter portion of our treatment period speaking with a power and a knowingness we did not even know was there when we began. Only those who have had such an experience will grasp just what is meant by this; but if you will follow the suggestions given in these lessons, they can lead to Oneness with God in consciousness, and you, yourself, will have this experience.

Treatment for Success

Everything within me is directed to success and fulfillment as I now let Divine Spirit motivate me in all my undertakings. Under Its government I may be certain to succeed. God works through man and among men, and His patterns of good I now accept as the patterns of my good.

Trust ye in the Lord for ever: for in the Lord Jehovah is everlasting strength. —Isaiah 26:4

WE CANNOT DEMONSTRATE BEYOND OUR ABILITY TO MENTALLY EMBODY AN IDEA. THE ARGUMENT IS BETWEEN OUR EXPERIENCE, WHAT THE WORLD BELIEVES, AND WHAT WE ARE CONVINCED IS THE TRUTH. —*The Science of Mind,* page 174

THE LAW AND THE WORD

One reason a person often finds it necessary to ask for professional practitioner help with a problem he has not been able to meet himself might be found in the "impersonality" with which a practitioner can *release* a treatment when the healing realization has been reached. The person whose problem it is, however, and even though he may reach as fine a realization in treatment as the practitioner would, will often be unable really to "let the word go," for he is personally too close to the problem and its appearance can be frightening, or seem impossible of solution.

If treatment is not released, it will be ineffective. The unplanted seed does not take root. It is of tremendous importance that we see the necessity of *releasing,* which is the sixth and concluding step in this treatment method. When you have spoken your word, bless it and let it go! Give thanks; in words of faith acknowledge that your word is now manifested, and express your gratitude to God—*and then shift your attention to something new.* Get up and *do* something else.

The word "Amen" in both Hebrew and Greek means *verily*—which means "in Truth." And this is what we mean when we end a treatment-prayer with the words so traditional in metaphysics: "And so it is!"

Treatment for Release of a Problem

I have spoken my word with sincerity. I declare that the answer is now mine. I affirm my faith in it and now I release the problem. I release myself utterly from it. I surrender it unto the Law that accomplishes all things, and I give myself wholly to the knowledge that it is now done. I accept the answer. And so it is.

Thy kingdom come. Thy will be done in earth, as it is in heaven.
—Matthew 6:10

When we treat we do not wish, we *know.* We do not dream, we *state.* We do not hope, we *accept. . . .* We do not expect something is going to happen, we *believe that it has already happened.* —*The Science of Mind,* page 399

A WORKING HYPOTHESIS

Every science has its working hypothesis. That of the Science of Mind goes something like this:

We believe that the Universe is a unity, not a chaos, and that all of the parts *within* It are part *of* It. This means, for us, that there is a responsible agency—God, Intelligence, Mind. The fact that order, purpose and direction are manifest in the parts implies that the primal Source creates in an orderly manner. Inasmuch as there is a personal potential within each of us, this potential must also be an aspect of *The Whole*. There is nothing else for it to be part of. This potential within man can be nothing other than God—the Divine Presence within us.

This can be reduced to a very simple proposition: (1) there is That which *knows*, and (2) there is the way It *works*.

Treatment is a methodical application of our working hypothesis to problems of individual or group good. In other words, on the assumption of Divine Mind as a present Reality is based our use of our own personal thought as a creative factor by which we may consciously affect our own destiny.

Having assumed this as a working hypothesis, we then discipline ourselves to work consciously with new thought patterns which embody the images of the good we have conceived and desire, and then observe whether the hypothesis proves itself in visible fact. *Does* thought change circumstance? We find that it does! All who put these lessons to use will prove our premise!

Treatment to Overcome Tension

I now release all thoughts of fear, anxiety, and strife. I accept that God's right action manifests in and through me and all my activities. I am properly guided in all that I do and harmony prevails in my affairs. My every endeavor is an activity filled with enthusiasm and joy.

Create in me a clean heart, O God; and renew a right spirit within me.
—Psalm 51:10

IN MENTAL TREATMENT WE SHOULD FEEL AS THOUGH THE WHOLE POWER OF THE UNIVERSE WERE RUNNING THROUGH THE WORDS WE SPEAK. —*The Science of Mind*, page 413

THE MEANING OF "HEARTFELT TREATMENT"

In the previous lesson we discussed "the science of our religion"; now we look at "the religion of our science."

It is good to grasp Principle with the intellect. *Knowledge is power.* It is even better to touch the Presence with the heart. *Love is happiness.*

God is as sweet as the grin on a shy boy's face, as lovely as a baby's touch with its little doll-like fingers. Man is made for such goodness. We are lonely until we have it in our grasp. Why do we want to cuddle the kitten, pat the puppy's head? Because we need to *touch* Life, not just to think about It!

Court the Presence, the wise teachers have said. Seek the Spirit within as a lover seeks love. The "hound of heaven" pursues the nearly awakened soul until at last he is ready to waken and to see that his life is One with God. This world is suddenly barren except we know that God is always with us. He becomes a living Presence, a Companion by our side, a Teacher in our home, a Helper with our burdens when we labor.

This is not mere poetic fancy. Both the cold facts of the intellect and the warmth of feeling in the heart are true. They are equally important. They are one truth, doubly described.

An intellectual treatment *will* have results. But a *heartfelt* treatment, released in joy, can bring a transcendent healing.

Treatment to Overcome Heartache

I turn to that Presence within which heals all hurts. I find there the Source of all peace and love. Whatever I may need is supplied by God's boundless love for His creation, of which I am a part. All the good things life doth hold, things that are beautiful and true, are mine to experience now.

––––––––––––

Though I speak with the tongues of men and of angels, and have not charity, I am become as sounding brass, or a tinkling cymbal.
—I Corinthians 13:1

ONLY LOVE KNOWS LOVE, AND LOVE KNOWS ONLY LOVE. WORDS CANNOT EXPRESS ITS DEPTH OR MEANING. A UNIVERSAL SENSE ALONE BEARS WITNESS TO THE DIVINE FACT: GOD IS LOVE AND LOVE IS GOD.
—*The Science of Mind*, page 478

SIMPLE AFFIRMATIONS

It has been said that the affirmation of real power is the spontaneous statement of realization that comes with the sudden seeing of a truth. For instance, a woman was to have a heart operation and told her practitioner the danger point would be when the surgeon would have to work by touch alone, not able to see what he was working with. He would be "working in the dark for five minutes," as he put it. The practitioner treated for some time without arriving at a full realization of "a perfect operation." But note that she *did treat*; and thus there was a place provided in consciousness *for* the realization. Then suddenly the words came into her mind: "God never works in the dark, even for five minutes!" With this, she had a full acceptance that "it was done," for God was in the surgeon's mind and hand. And it was indeed so, as events proved.

In our discovery of transcendent and wordless consciousness, we should never underestimate the power of such simple human affirmations. Most of us have favorite statements which have come to possess almost a miraculous value, for they have meant so much to us, time and again when we felt in need.

Essentially, treatment is not time spent, words used, method or non-method, but rather the actual rearrangement in consciousness of patterns of thought. When consciousness is changed, treatment is effective.

Some Treatment Affirmations

I am One with the undivided One! There is One Life, that Life is God, that Life is my life now. God is my help in every need, perfect Spirit, perfectly present. There is instant right action, right now; and regardless of appearances, my good is now flowing to me. Thank you, God, that it is done!

By the word of truth, by the power of God, by the armour of righteousness on the right hand and on the left.   —II Corinthians 6:7

THE PRACTITIONER WORKS WITHIN HIS OWN MIND UNTIL HE IS MENTALLY SATISFIED, UNTIL THE WHOLE REACTION IN HIS THOUGHT CAUSES HIM TO UNDERSTAND THAT HIS PATIENT IS NOW HEALED.

—*The Science of Mind*, page 409

CONTEMPLATION

We have been dealing with spiritual mind treatment as a specific "thing to be done, for an identifiable purpose." We hope this point has been clearly established. But the scope of spiritual mind treatment goes far beyond this, of course. So let us mention two more areas of spiritual adventure which one should investigate and experience.

The first is *contemplation,* which has two basic aspects: *contemplation outward,* where one directs his consciousness toward those parts of God's creation; and *contemplation inward,* where one turns within himself, enriched by the vision the first stage has made possible, and discovers within himself that same glory of creation he perceived outside himself.

Unless you can contemplate and recognize God-Life in a tree, in a leaf, in a bird, or whatever you may choose, you can never wholly recognize that God is also the Life within you.

Love is itself the only gateway to love. When did you last take time just to sit in your garden and look at it? There was a woman who had lived for twenty years under two glorious pine trees which she had never really noticed until she developed a new outlook on life.

Contemplation trains the mind in the arts of *stillness* and of *seeing* and they provide a foundation for spiritual healing treatment.

Meditation on the Miracle of Life

At the center of all that lives, "nestles the seed, perfection." The ancient sea and all therein, the hills and their creatures, the sky and the stars—I contemplate all and directly know the Presence of God within them! And then I feel the miracle of my own heartbeat.

But if from thence thou shalt seek the Lord thy God, thou shalt find him, if thou seek him with all thy heart, and with all thy soul.
—Deuteronomy 4:29

ALL EMERGE FROM THAT ONE WHOSE BEING IS EVER PRESENT AND WHOSE LIFE, ROBED IN NUMBERLESS FORMS, IS MANIFEST THROUGHOUT ALL CREATION. —*The Science of Mind,* page 420

DEVOTIONAL PRAYER

Another area of spiritual experience which should not be overlooked is that of *devotional prayer*. It means exactly what the words imply: *talking to God with praise and humility.*

All forms of thought which endeavor to recognize man's unity with God are some form of prayer, and of these one of the sweetest is that kind of prayer in which we have neither need nor inquiry, neither desire nor search, but only communion, pure and sweet—and completely personal! You cannot pray in this manner unless you believe in a God you can talk to.

Did not Jesus say "After this manner pray ye: 'Our Father' . . . ."? And with the words that follow give us the greatest prayer in history?

There are many classic treatises on devotional prayer—such books as *The Cloud of Unknowing, The Imitation of Christ, Theologica Germanica,* and *Meister Eckhart.* These books acquaint one with God, the Father. And how far shall we get, without a sense of our Sonship?

One modern servant of the Father says that while Divine healing is important and needful, "Divine living" is what we should want! Devotional prayer is the greatest single path to this awareness, and it can bring healing where all else has not availed!

A Prayer of Praise

"I am that which Thou art, Thou art that which I am." All that I am, all that I can be, my every hope, aspiration, and good desire spring from your Life at the center of my being. For this understanding I give thanks, and now permit myself to be a fuller channel for the expression of all that You are. I honor Thee by becoming more like Thee.

By him therefore let us offer the sacrifice of praise to God continually, that is, the fruit of our lips giving thanks to his name.

—Hebrews 13:15

ALMIGHTY GOD, EVERLASTING GOOD, ETERNAL SPIRIT, MAKER OF ALL THINGS, AND KEEPER OF MY LIFE, THOU ART ALL.

—*The Science of Mind,* page 549

HIGH VISION

As we finish this section of our lessons in spiritual mind treatment, let us think along these lines:

Because God is Wholeness, unhealthiness need not continue. Because God is Peace, confusion is never enduring. Because God is Love, no inharmony can prevail. Because God is all, no poverty is real. We may pass through the cloud of unknowing or the night of pain, but *God has not failed!* He is there. He is present now. He is our Source. His Sons we are, His daughters. In us is the Christ-spirit; we are the children of the living God.

In the instant of seeing, we are restored. Let us know with David: "He restoreth my soul; he leadeth me in paths of righteousness for his name's sake." Let us cling to high vision, for the visions we conceive must become our capacities. The place where our attention is, is the place of power. That to which we submit becomes our master.

And no man can serve two masters. Do we believe that God can heal? Then let us believe in God!

We put faith in too many things! Faith in one thing will prevail over faith divided. Let us place our faith in the Power that made us, that dwells in us now, that *is* the only truth, the only fact, the only real thing.

And let us *give voice to our faith!* Our word will not return to us void.

Meditation on "High Vision"

The highest God and the innermost God is One God. God, the Source of all things, is also that which I am. God's creative activity in me now reaches a point where I can recognize Him for all that He is. As my mind opens up in this new awareness I know that I am in the One, and all is complete and perfect.

Continue in prayer, and watch in the same with thanksgiving.
—Colossians 4:2

WE NOW LET GO OF EVERYTHING AND ENTER INTO THE CONTEMPLATION OF PEACE AND GOOD AND TRUTH AND BEAUTY. WE ARE CONSCIOUS THAT GOD IS ALL THERE IS, THERE IS NOTHING ELSE.
—*The Science of Mind,* page 562

SECTION TWO

Methods of Treatment in the Science of Mind
for Various Human Problems of a Specific Nature

INTRODUCTION—II

The lessons in this section deal with special problems and circumstances which are likely to confront anyone.

The material alternates between an analysis of the problem from the viewpoint of the Science of Mind (in light type), and a personalized example (in bold type) of what you may then declare for yourself as the healing truth about the problem. The analysis outlines the reasoning behind the healing idea; the suggested statement of personal application provides a channel in consciousness through which the thought will operate in a healing manner. *And it will do so,* because a "treatment given is a Law set into motion." It is the certainty of this fact—rather than its being the whimsical or capricious act of an on-again, off-again God—that makes the application of the principles of Science of Mind a true science.

Your individual mind is a part of the Universal Mind, and therefore when you think, Universal Mind is thinking, and *the Law of Mind has been moved into action!* You put this Law into action, scientifically and in a definite way, whenever you choose to do so (or when you remember to!). But most of the time, you probably go through your days more or less automatically and uncreatively, reaping a crop of previously sown thought-seeds. However, each event in which you participate—regardless of how habitual or automatic it may be—had a cause, and each cause had a thought behind it. And if you are not accustomed to directing your thoughts constructively, you are likely to be caught up in a series of such cause-and-effect chains which make certain things (usually bad ones) seem inevitable and inescapable.

But this unrecognized yielding to the bondage of automatic cause-and-effect can cease immediately, the "karmic" shackles can be cast away, when you discover how *consciously* to use the Law of Mind through spiritual mind treatment, rather than habitually using the Law in ignorance of what you are actually doing to yourself.

Spiritual mind treatment, then, involves deliberately inducing constructive thought within the medium of Universal Mind, which in Its creative function as Law, tends to produce in the outer world an equivalent of the inner thought.

It is an *art*—a skill which can be learned and taught.

It is an *act*—something that is done, and is not done until you do it.

It is a *science*—a technique that operates in accordance with definite Law.

Spiritual mind treatment is a recognition of and an agreement with the Divinity which indwells mankind. It is, in fact, affirmative prayer, spoken forth in a scientific manner and in faith, believing. As you come to understand that the tangible world of personal experience is the outpicturing of mental equivalents, you realize that when wrong ideas are replaced with right ones, you become whole. When mistaken or limited belief is replaced with true concepts and an unlimited acceptance of God's Perfect Life within you, you are healed. When, in this manner, you touch that inner world of Divine Perfection, affirming your oneness with It, you understand at last and may truly pronounce in all honesty that most basic and powerful of metaphysical affirmations: THERE IS ONE LIFE. THAT LIFE IS GOD. THAT LIFE IS PERFECT. THAT LIFE IS MY LIFE NOW.

Prayer, or treatment, is the aligning of your individual thought with the perfect right action of God. But you cannot pray successfully for abundance (for example) while continuing to entertain the subconscious belief in poverty which caused your original difficulty. You cannot accept something in your mind and have it coexist with a habitual picture of the opposite, and so acceptance of something you *choose* is likely also to involve a letting-go of a contrary way of thinking which you have embraced habitually. This need to abandon previous patterns of thinking is likely to manifest in the form of a struggle either in your thought or in your life, but you must clearly understand that the struggle is between yourself and yourself. There is no devil whom you must fight. There is no eternal principle of negation or of evil which you must battle. And most importantly, there is no reluctance on the part of God for you to overcome, for the only barriers to well-being are within yourself. God is God, and will continue to be so. What you must do is to bring your own thought into alignment with God's Nature within you if you are to experience It fully.

You should take time each day to turn to God, surrendering every discord, every sense of limitation. You are a Divine Being on the pathway of eternal Good. *Say* so! "Thrust in thy sickle..." Claim your inheritance. Does the Son have to approach his Father with apology? Jesus thought not. In his parable, he said that when the prodigal son came back at last to his father's home and proclaimed himself unworthy, the father did not even reply to his protestations but called for the robe and the calf. . . .

Whether for psychological or for religious reasons, and whatever your persuasion may be, take this book and these lessons and prove them now, seeing if they will not truly change your life!

A MEDITATION FOR STILLNESS AND KNOWING

Slip quietly into an atmosphere of absolute stillness. Be still. Quiet is within you. Just be still. Then affirm:

My life is of God. In quietness I know that His Spirit is indeed the life within me. God lives and moves and has some part of His infinite Being in me! I reflect upon this idea. I let it become something I know with true conviction.

At the center of everything there is a pool of Peace from which quietude and harmony and healing proceed. Behind every human anxiety there is the right solution waiting to be expressed. Go back to the consciousness of God within you in your meditation now, and know that here at the center of your life you have access to that Wisdom which is able to guide you in the experience of wholeness and perfection as you rely upon It.

I enter in consciousness, now, that place of the Most High and abide in the awareness of God's Presence. I am receptive to the Wisdom which gives me the knowledge to bring harmony and right action into every phase of my daily living.

With deep and solemn conviction, know there is that within you which is God's own Presence and which will tell you of Itself. "Be still, and know that I am God," is the great admonition.

I now understand the great prayer of the ages: "I am that which Thou art, Thou art that which I am." Truly am I established in the Wise and the Good.

————————

The Lord is righteous in all his ways, and holy in all his works.
                                                    —Psalm 145:17

GOD IS AN IMMEDIATE PRESENCE AND AN IMMEDIATE EXPERIENCE IN MY MIND AND SOUL, AND I AM CONSCIOUS OF THIS PERFECT PRESENCE, THIS DIVINE WISDOM, THIS ETERNAL WHOLENESS.
                                    —*The Science of Mind,* page 559

TRUSTING THE UNIVERSE

Always, God is the answer. In Divine Love and Wisdom are the answers to all of man's problems. Let your prayer or treatment awaken within you the acceptance of the answer to take the place of the problem. You should expect to receive, and should *accept now,* a perfect working-out of whatever troubles you have. Say:

In a consciousness of Divine Oneness, I now speak my word for the resolving of the particular problem that concerns me. No need is too small or too great for infinite Intelligence to meet. I turn my attention to that inner Source and receive Its guiding action.

Whether your problem is one that concerns your personal health or decisions regarding your business affairs or the welfare of members of your family, always God is the answer. Always there is the Wisdom that makes right and sure your way when you choose to permit It and to follow It. Continue to know:

There is no power opposed to God. There is no truth outside of God. I know therefore that nothing can impede the right action that follows for me as the result of this positive word of faith. I contemplate now the perfect picture of its outward expression. I enter into the joy of it. My trust in God is unshakable.

Now quietly release your word and bless it unto its accomplishment. It will go on working for you, and you will know what your answer is at the right moment, and in the right manner.

For every one that asketh, receiveth; and he that seeketh, findeth; and to him that knocketh it shall be opened. —Luke 11:10

When we learn to trust the Universe, we shall be happy, prosperous and well. —*The Science of Mind,* page 33

PERSONAL REASSURANCE

To build a life upon sure foundations and to know the "fruits" of wholesome endeavors, turn your thoughts from the confusion and wrongness of personal and world conditions. Seek your reassurance daily from the Source of the only true power that can heal the affairs of man. Say:

I turn from the conditions and people which are disturbing me, and seek now to realize God's Presence as the only power in my affairs and in my relationships. I face myself honestly and am willing to change. I want to do good and to receive only good. I let God's Love begin with me and penetrate every relationship, and I hereby prepare myself to do my part in all the ways that daily living demands of me.

Know that there is nothing in you to resist God's perfect Life in any form. Develop a nonresistance to the Life of God in you, in your family, in your friends, and in your business relationships. Let your real Self salute the real Self in every person with whom you deal. Continue your treatment for this understanding:

I believe that all people partake of the One Life. I put my faith completely in the indwelling Spirit and look to It alone for the strength to build my life wisely and well. I now give thanks that this faith in God's eternal Goodness in the heart of man restores my confidence and increases my understanding.

And they shall build houses and inhabit them; and they shall plant vineyards, and eat the fruit of them. —Isaiah 65:21

UNDERSTANDING ALONE CONSTITUTES TRUE SALVATION, EITHER HERE OR HEREAFTER. —*The Science of Mind,* page 383

RIGHT RELATIONSHIPS

A failure to communicate generally goes with relationship failures. Where communication breaks down, *all* the people involved—including you—are at fault, regardless of any factors or circumstances. People fail to communicate harmoniously with one another because somewhere they have failed in their communication with God. Think silently of your relationship to God. Does man create himself? Is life a bodily thing only, or is it of Spirit? Is God the Father of *all*? Even of those in your relationship problems? Begin your self-treatment by pronouncing your belief in God. Say:

I believe in God. I know that with God all things are possible. Regardless of yesterday's errors I am forgiven as I forgive. The Divine in me and in these others shows us that which is perfect and good, right now and completely.

Silently realize that although every person is a part of the One Life, each expresses Life at the level of his own understanding, and so do you. But, while someone may seek to instruct you and to help you, you are the only person who can really change your understanding and bring it into agreement with God's Perfection. Do this, and you will help others as well.

I really do want peace and right understanding to prevail in my affairs. I stop justifying my own position and let the inner Spirit bring me into harmonious activity. I know that this does not depend upon person, place, or thing. It is born out of my willingness to practice the Presence of God!

Bless them that persecute you: bless, and curse not.
—Romans 12:14

WHEN THE INNER CONSCIOUSNESS AGREES WITH THE TRUTH, THEN—AND NOT UNTIL THEN—A DEMONSTRATION TAKES PLACE.
—*The Science of Mind,* page 236

40

LEGAL CASES

The essential thing to know in lawsuits or other legal cases is that there is no testimony higher than the truth. Truth declared through every facet of a case can bring justice into a courtroom right through every appearance of human limitation. It can change an entire atmosphere; and if something needs to be brought out, it will be, in spite of any effort to impede it! Treat like this:

I accept that the truth is operating in this case now, and moving within the litigants, judge, jury, and attorneys. Truth reveals itself. Justice proclaims itself, and is established. I accept now that Divine action, right action, is the only action in this case and that the truth is manifest.

One never treats to win a case, but only along the above lines. One must never mentally try to coerce others in a spiritual mind treatment; but one must always proclaim and accept that Divine action eliminates every barrier to the expression of the truth. Sometimes justice is not exactly apparent; there are very few one-sided cases in our courts! One could not use prayer to harm another, or to "conquer" another person, but only to accept and experience the truth. From it alone can good come. Man receives no acquittal from the acts of his consciousness, and an early confession of error or wrongdoing would mean an earlier restitution to his own good and to freedom.

For so is the will of God, that with well-being ye may put to silence the ignorance of foolish men: As free, and not using your liberty for a cloak of maliciousness, but as the servants of God. —I Peter 2:15-16

EVERY MAN MUST PAY THE PRICE FOR THAT WHICH HE RECEIVES AND THAT PRICE IS PAID IN MENTAL AND SPIRITUAL COIN.
—*The Science of Mind,* page 268

THE LONELINESS PROBLEM

Loneliness can be a real problem, and it does no good for someone just to say, "Oh, pull yourself together and cheer up! Stop feeling sorry for yourself!" If it were that easy we would not have a loneliness problem to begin with! But one might begin treatment for oneself this way:

I know that I am healed of whatever lies behind my loneliness—be it timidity, lack of self-confidence, selfishness, self-centeredness, or any other cause. I am no longer alone and sorry for myself, and I now start to live a life that is happy and joyful. Regardless of my present situation, as I begin now to change my thoughts and my emotional reactions to it, my new patterns of thinking establish for me that which I desire.

Now let us think for a moment about right companionship. For it to come into our lives, we must start knowing that it exists for us, regardless of present appearances. Take it up in treatment this way:

I believe that for each person there are right companions and right friends; and that there is right companionship for me, too. I believe this is an established fact, right now. This prayer is as a seed planted and will result in the actual experience of such companionship and true friends, for I know that God, the Father of all, meets all of my needs, and I give thanks.

Thou hast made known to me the ways of life; thou shalt make me full of joy with thy countenance.   —Acts 2:28

THOUGHTS ARE MORE THAN THINGS, THEY ARE THE CAUSE OF THINGS.
                    —*The Science of Mind,* page 414

EMPLOYMENT

Here is a good basic treatment for employment:

There is a right job for me, and I claim it now. It is mine because I am just the one for it. Somehow, and in the right way, God is bringing me and that job together, now!

Some people want a new type of work or career. They could treat:

I am sane of mind, sound of body, ready, willing, and able to serve God better in a new position or in a new line of work. I accept right now the wisdom of Divine Intelligence and I have faith that I am guided in the action I am to take. Thank you, Father, for this new position.

Women sometimes have "hurdles" to overcome. Treat in this way:

In Divine Mind there is never any impediment to perfect right action. I accept this as the law for me in my finding the right place of employment. I am not bound by human thoughts of limitation. There is the right and wonderful work for me, and I gratefully accept it.

Perhaps your need is for right workers or employees. Treat along these lines:

Exactly the right person for the job I have to offer is on the way, right now! My business is God's business and He supplies the employee I need. He endows me with the wisdom and understanding to be a good employer. I give thanks for the fulfillment of my need.

If ye be willing and obedient, ye shall eat the good of the land.
—Isaiah 1:19

. . . THE MAN WHOSE CONSCIOUSNESS IS NOW BRINGING HIM A SMALLER THING OR A LESS IMPORTANT THING . . . CAN IF HE DESIRES CONCEIVE THE BIGGER THING. . . .

—*The Science of Mind,* page 287

PRAYING FOR A "MIRACLE" TO HAPPEN!

From time to time a problem presents itself and it seems that only a "miracle" could solve it. Very well, let us know that the miraculous does happen, but at the same time realize that what appears to us as miraculous is but the normal, natural action of the Law of God. Law can never be violated, but It can be directed into new and different ways. Realize that "a miracle is a natural event in a spiritual world." Say, then, to yourself:

In the consciousness that nothing is outside of the Divine Power to heal and set right, I accept your guidance, God, in whatever steps I must take. My faith is in your Wisdom and Its action within all concerned. I let no other thought contradict it.

Perhaps you have been wondering where problems come from, if all there is is God? Or you may have been thinking that since your life is some part of God's Life—and God could not be sick or confused or out of harmony—how could you be in this difficulty? Only by virtue of the wrong use—perhaps unconsciously—of the creative power of your own thought and your power of choice! So you must get your muddled thinking out of the way and let God's infinite Intelligence express Itself fully in your experience.

Whatever aspect of my experience needs a "miracle" to correct it, I now know that it is corrected through the normal natural action of Divine Intelligence. I affirm and accept this action as taking place now.

Commit thy way unto the Lord; trust also in him; and he shall bring it to pass. —Psalm 37:5

WE ARE SURROUNDED BY AN INFINITE POSSIBILITY. . . . WE SHOULD HAVE FAITH IN IT, AND ITS DESIRES AND ITS ABILITY TO DO FOR US ALL THAT WE SHALL EVER NEED TO HAVE DONE.
—*The Science of Mind,* page 46

NERVOUS CONDITIONS

It is one of the miracles of Life that the human body contains a marvelous nervous system which enables us to become sensitive to the world about us—physically, mentally, and spiritually. Nervous illness often is due not to a sick body, but to a wrong mental adjustment to people and to conditions of daily living. Absolute peace of mind would heal such illness instantly. The rooting out of antagonisms would heal it. Begin treatment in this way:

Deliberately, sincerely, and quietly I turn from the outer world, and my reactions to it, to the inner world of Spirit—to the center of God's Life within me—for I know I could not be alive without It. It is the center of Peace, of Order, of Beauty, and of Love, and I align myself with these aspects of Life and know that all of my reactions to conditions about me are controlled by these qualities.

The person with a "nervous" problem should recognize that excessive self-concern is at the root of most of his troubles, and that, as he becomes more God-centered, he will become more love-centered, more other-people-centered at the same time. His whole system responds to this more wholesome outlook, enabling him to function more effectively and beneficially. Say:

I do first things first and move untroubled, without strain or tension, from one task to another. I am no longer in bondage to past patterns of thinking. Today I walk through my world at peace with it. I recognize the wonder of Life within all people, and give thanks.

. . . the Lord is the strength of my life; of whom shall I be afraid?
—Psalm 27:1

RIGHT THOUGHT, CONSTANTLY POURED INTO CONSCIOUSNESS, WILL EVENTUALLY PURIFY IT.   *—The Science of Mind,* page 204

CHILDREN

The important thing to realize is that your child is a child of God. He came to and through you, but his life is not of your making. Divine Intelligence within this child can do anything that needs to be done and is endeavoring to do it *now*. Give your recognition only to God-Life. Say:

Regardless of the outer appearance, I do know that the life within my child is God's Life individualized. This Life is subject to no law other than Its own Perfection, and I accept this expression in and through my child right now.

However, you must remember that your child responds to the atmosphere you create in your home; to your emotions of love and hate, joy and anger; to the good as well as to the bad. The chances are that you need to heal yourself, perhaps, of an unconscious expression of negative emotions; otherwise, your child will continue to be subject to illness or difficulty. Do it now:

I accept right now the absolute Wisdom and Love and Peace that make me a true channel for God's complete expression in our home. I let whatever needs healing in me be healed, so that nothing remains in my consciousness to hinder my child's happy experience in living.

Where doctors or nurses are involved, know that Divine Intelligence is guiding them to do exactly the right thing. Release your word in trust; let go and *let* God!

Be ye doers of the word, and not hearers only. . . .   —James 1:22

. . . IT IS THE BUSINESS OF THE PRACTITIONER TO REALIZE THAT THERE IS NO MENTAL INFLUENCE OPERATING THROUGH THE CHILD EXCEPT A BELIEF IN PERFECTION.   —*The Science of Mind,* page 211

PROSPERITY

Prosperity is an "absolute." There is no such thing as "greater prosperity." There is such a thing as more money or less money; but prosperity is having the money we need when we need it! Speak your word for prosperity in this way:

I recognize a Divine sufficiency as constant in all my affairs. I live in a universe of abundance. There is plenty of everything. I believe it. I also believe that the Source that supplies the world with its abundance supplies me with mine!

Pause in your treatment and silently contemplate this wonderful idea. God's world and your world comprise a unity. Begin to realize that you need let nothing in your thinking or feeling interfere with the right flowing to you of all your good, and this of course includes money. You are healed of any mental block or emotional bias right now! Make your affirmations and gratefully accept your good.

I know that there is no power opposed to God! My substance, my supply, all that is enriching flows to me from the eternal Source. My expectancy is of God and this prayer engages the creative power of fulfillment. Something has actually changed in my consciousness as I put my trust unequivocally in God's action in my life. My prosperity is really set into motion in a most wonderful way. It is done, and I give thanks.

Bless the Lord, O my soul, and forget not all his benefits.

—Psalm 103:2

OUR MENTAL ACCEPTANCES SHOULD BE FILLED WITH CONVICTION, WARMTH, COLOR AND IMAGINATION. THE CREATIVE POWER RESPONDS TO FEELING MORE QUICKLY THAN TO ANY OTHER MENTAL ATTITUDE.
—*The Science of Mind,* page 398

CHANGING CONDITIONS

Is it time for a change? While there is a principle which indicates that we must change ourselves rather than try to change other people, it does not mean that there are never times when we are *not* in the right place for us, or with the people we should *not* be with. If this is your feeling, begin treatment in this way:

I am completely willing to change myself if there is something in me which is keeping me in an unhappy environment. I am also willing to do the things which make for happiness, now, where I am, as the beginning step of moving toward my greater good. If my service to God and man can be improved by a change in my work, my home, or my general environment, I will be rightly guided into such a change, and I welcome it.

We should understand that changes take place first in the personal response of the individual to the conditions in which he finds himself. However, we do find some things more conducive to constructive endeavor and to general well-being than others; and we have the right as well as the duty to live life pleasantly and creatively. Realizing this, continue with the treatment:

I know that I exist in an eternal state of unity with my God and with all of Life, and that I may always expect good, as I align myself with it. I give thanks for the guidance which takes me where I should be. I move forward willingly, trustfully, and with complete peace of mind.

Blessed are they which do hunger and thirst after righteousness: for they shall be filled. —Matthew 5:6

THE UNIVERSE IS FOOLPROOF. . . . WE MUST EXPECT TO EXPERIENCE THE LOGICAL RESULT OF OUR THOUGHT AND ACT, BE IT GOOD OR WHAT WE CALL EVIL. —*The Science of Mind,* page 110

TEENAGERS

Adolescence is a perfectly normal and natural part of everybody's development. Everything that goes with it is equally natural. Not always understandable, and sometimes slightly nerve-racking, but an inevitable segment of experience. After all, it is God's Life that is seeking expression. Let us give It a chance, shall we? Say:

I salute the God-self in our wonderful teenager, and I know that Divine Love protects and Divine Wisdom instructs and guides him (her) now and always. I have faith in God, so I have faith in God in my child. I know that each young person must learn what Life has to teach. Each one is unique. Each must do his own living; each has a right to express. And I know that my child is rightly guided in expressing the highest concepts of Life.

Parents must be a bulwark of strength, understanding and sympathy, never demeaning the adolescent's problems, never underestimating the importance of "trivial" things to a young person. We must guide, instruct when needed, try not to interfere unduly, or impose standards of adulthood too soon; yet, encourage normal steady maturity, independence, and high goals. Above all, we must not worry! Our part is to accept the spiritual Truth, and cling to It in the face of any challenge, and say:

This is God's perfect child, growing up now into perfect adulthood, in a perfect way! Thank you, Father of all!

Train up a child in the way he should go: and when he is old, he will not depart from it. —Proverbs 22:6

A REALIZATION OF THE PRESENCE OF GOD IS THE MOST POWERFUL HEALING AGENCY KNOWN TO THE MIND OF MAN.
—*The Science of Mind*, page 145

FORGIVENESS

Life is right now, forever! Our living is always *now*. We cannot live a minute from now. We cannot relive the minute that has just passed; we can only recapture it as a memory, if we choose to do this. Yesterday happened, and it was what it was. But living is *now,* and God's Love is the only law of our being. Say:

I concede that anything I did yesterday—in all my yesterdays—I did because that was the best I understood at the time. If it was wrong, it was due to my ignorance only. I knew no better, and so acted upon the knowledge and understanding I had. Today I look in reverence to Him who gives the day and to His guidance for each moment. I forgive myself, and I forgive my fellowmen for their trespasses, and I accept God's loving forgiveness for my mistakes.

Instead of spending time dwelling upon past mistakes, realize that it can be spent far more creditably, far more constructively, in dwelling upon what is now eternally right and good for you and for others. Say:

I know that the God-Life indwelling me will establish those conditions of good which I seek with complete sincerity of mind and heart. I let my thought be in harmony with It. I give thanks for this wonderful new beginning my prayer of acceptance makes possible for me.

For if ye forgive men their trespasses, your heavenly Father will also forgive you. —Matthew 6:14

WHAT A LOAD IS DROPPED FROM THE SHOULDERS OF PERSONAL RESPONSIBILITY, WHEN WE REALIZE THAT THE ETERNAL MIND HOLDS NAUGHT AGAINST ANYONE. —*The Science of Mind,* page 457

PEACE OF MIND

You must come to know that you are some part of the great Reality and that you have been given tremendous power in governing your life and experiences through the creative power of your thought. For the most part you have probably been using this power in ignorance and therefore thoughts of hate and fear and anxiety have brought you unhappy experiences. But, just as easily, thoughts of love and compassion could have brought you happy ones. Say aloud:

Today, I beneficially use for good this power of creativity, and bring all of my ideas into the realm of constructive thinking. Fear, guilt, and any sense of rejection are not the nature of Reality, but the result of my own misunderstanding of God's Presence in me and in others.

Peace of mind comes from awareness of this Presence, of Its Love and Wisdom within you—real and wonderful and always personal to you. Accept right now and right where you are, the healing of doubt, of fear, and of all negative reactions to the world around you. Cease to be bothered by what doesn't matter —only God matters! Say:

I let go all else and concern myself with the things of God so that I may express them intelligently from now on. I am filled with the Peace that is of God.

. . . let him take hold of my strength, that he may make peace with me, and he shall make peace with me. —Isaiah 27:5

WE CANNOT BE IN PEACE UNTIL WE KNOW THAT THE SPIRIT IS THE ONLY CAUSE, MEDIUM AND EFFECT IN OUR LIVES. . . . EVIL HAS NO HISTORY AND HAS NEVER ENTERED IN TO THE BEING OR THE EXPERIENCE OF REALITY. —*The Science of Mind,* page 264

MENTAL STABILITY

Every neurosis is the result of a person's developing, for one reason or another, an unnatural self-concern or attention to something, or in some way isolating himself from normal, happy relationships with other people. Say to yourself:

The time has come that I now want healing and wholesome reactions to life more than I want this mental disturbance. God did not give it to me; and it is time for me to stop blaming other people for it, too. I let it go for it has no place in my life.

If you believe this, you have begun your healing. Are you ready to be honest with yourself? This is the one essential thing. You could not be neurotic if you were not being dishonest somewhere! (And resistance to this statement, incidentally, is a neurosis speaking.) The spiritual *you* is yearning for you to be honest, healthy, and normal. Try cooperating with this real Self. The healing of a neurosis is fostered when you sincerely seek a better way to express Life than the one you have been using. Continue to affirm:

I now turn within to discover a higher, better way of life. I cast aside my pretenses, my petty self-concerns, my unworthy thoughts. I am restored to the paths of righteousness—right-useness—as I am completely honest with myself. Under God's loving guidance, I cannot fail. I am grateful for this restoration to stability.

Cast away from you all your transgressions, whereby ye have transgressed; and make you a new heart and a new spirit. . . .
—Ezekiel 18:31

It is probable that when Jesus forgave the man his sins, he realized that the man had a complex of condemnation within himself.   —*The Science of Mind,* page 237

GETTING OUT OF TROUBLE

So you are in trouble again! But you want to get out. You do not like your trouble, and are willing to let it go! Turn now to That which is forever untroubled. Affirm along these lines:

I realize now that the only true restorative power in man's life is of God. The answer to my need, the meeting of my want, the restoration of my experiences to wholesomeness, now comes as I turn to and accept the infinite Love and untroubled Wisdom of God.

In this treatment remove from your mental atmosphere the fears, doubts, or other negative beliefs which have brought you into trouble, and place into the atmosphere of your personal beliefs a faith in God to guide and sustain your life in harmony and wholesome activities. Continue:

I am getting out of trouble right now, even as I speak, for I have moved already into the atmosphere of the Reality of my being. I give entrance into my experience to that good which harms no one and brings me into real happiness. I release the negative through forgiveness, and accept the good in gratitude. Thank you, God, that it is done!

Infinite Harmony and Love and Wisdom are within you. Use them as the basis of your living from now on.

———————————

The Lord is nigh unto all them that call upon him, to all that call upon him in truth. —Psalm 145:18

THE ONE WHO WISHES TO DEMONSTRATE SOME PARTICULAR GOOD MUST BECOME CONSCIOUS OF THIS PARTICULAR GOOD, IF HE WISHES TO EXPERIENCE IT. —*The Science of Mind,* page 46

ACCIDENT CASES

A quick and fervent affirmation of the Presence and Power of God is essential in treating accident cases. Whatever the accident—a cut finger, bruised toe, or the more serious results of a traffic collision—turning the attention to God's healing Power immediately calls forth Its manifestation. You turn from the confusion, emotional stress, or the inattentiveness that caused the mishap and identify yourself with the pattern of Perfection within, which is not subject to damage but forever sustains Itself in perfect form. Say:

Nothing can happen to the Divine plan of my body-temple. There is no hurt, damage, break, or pain in it. The powerful Life-force within me is right now flowing through every part of my body, renewing and restoring it in accord with its perfect pattern. I am grateful.

Suppose a friend has had an accident and you want to offer healing treatment. Say something like this:

I speak my word in the knowledge that God's Power is the whole and complete Power in my friend. Regardless of human opinion, Its action right now renews and revitalizes each part affected by the accident, and restores it to perfect health as though no accident had occurred! The Love of God heals all mental confusion and every apprehension pertaining to this situation. This I believe and accept. Thank you, God.

The Lord is my shepherd; I shall not want.　　　　　—Psalm 23:1

. . . WE SEE THERE CAN BE NO LIMIT TO THE POWER TO HEAL, OTHER THAN THE LIMIT OF OUR ABILITY TO CONCEIVE THAT POWER AS HEALING.　　　　　—*The Science of Mind*, page 197

REAL ESTATE TRANSACTIONS

Spiritual mind treatment can be effective in the case of buying or selling property, as in all other departments of normal living; but in real estate the problem is often one of *time.* There is a pattern of delay in the race consciousness which should be overcome. You could begin treatment this way:

Believing in Divine action, I affirm that there is no obstruction or delay in the proper conclusion of my business transactions. To the best of my knowledge, and in good faith, I believe that the transaction I am now concerned with is one of good for all parties involved. This good is established right now, and right action takes place now.

One must have an open mind in real estate affairs. Home owners almost never correctly evaluate their own property, because of sentiment. "This is my home!" Well, to the buyer, it is a house for sale. Until you accept this, you have not emotionally released the house, and can blame no one if it does not sell! If you really want to sell your house, then release it completely, become quite impersonal about it. Get the right estimate of its value from a reputable agent, and go to work in treatment for right action, right now. Include your acceptance of your own new house, if this is involved. Really feel eager to be in the new home! Don't linger! Speak the word, like this:

Thank you, God, that the right buyer for my house is here, right now. He loves it, and wants it, and pays for it! Thank you for the new home that I now accept as mine.

. . . What things soever ye desire, when ye pray, believe that ye receive them, and ye shall have them. —Mark 11:24

No good can come to us unless it make its advent through the center of God-Consciousness which we are.
—*The Science of Mind,* page 415

PHYSICAL HEALTH

The spiritual body, in God's image and likeness, is always whole. Physical health is its *natural* expression in the outer form. But too often we block the free flow of Life through the body-temple by our ignorant use of the creative power of thought. Pain and suffering are actual experiences, but we believe that they are due to misuse of the Laws of Being and are not God-ordained. Say:

I give up every harmful thought, false belief, and negative emotion that has kept me in the bondage of illness. I now let myself be Divinely guided to think and to do the things that establish me in wholeness and well-being.

Remember that a spiritual mind treatment is to establish in you a consciousness of the Source of your being. Turn your attention from the condition which you desire to change and begin to realize that there is only God's Life; that Life is Perfect; that Life is your life now. Let your thought dwell on this truth and embody it. Say:

God's Life is not subject to disease, pain, impairment, or malfunction. My body is vibrant with this Life. Every cell, nerve, sinew, and organ is Divine Substance, functioning in accord with the Divine plan of my body-temple, and I am now in mental agreement with It. I let it be done in love and in understanding.

Within your physical form right now is the Life-principle able to heal you and to restore you as though you had never been unwell! Give It a chance by believing in It.

O Lord of hosts, blessed is the man that trusteth in thee.
—Psalm 84:12

SCIENTIFIC MENTAL HEALING . . . IS A SYSTEMATIC PROCESS OF REASONING, WHICH UNEARTHS THE MENTAL CAUSE OR IDEA UNDERLYING DISEASE, AND PRESENTS THE TRUTH ABOUT MAN'S BEING.
—*The Science of Mind*, page 203

IN THE CASE OF AN OPERATION

Many who believe sincerely in Divine healing feel it is a compromise to seek medical aid. Yet, when those who love us are upset because they think a professional expert should be consulted, we should be willing to solicit that opinion. Say:

Under Divine guidance I take those steps that will be for my highest good. I accept all the knowledge that will help me in re-establishing my body-temple in health. God's Love and Wisdom sustain me and all who minister to me.

We seek advice from many agencies that help us with other problems. And when a physical condition does not seem to be met through prayer alone, we should not hesitate to use any and all channels of Wisdom to alleviate it. The doctor's intelligence and skill stem from God, too; and he is of great service to man. Sometimes a surgeon's skill is called into play. Treat along these lines:

I have absolute peace of mind about this operation. I know that Divine Intelligence guides the decisions of all involved. It also guides the surgeon's hand and expresses through the attendants' and nurses' care. An atmosphere of love and security embrace me and the Divine restorative action of Life manifests in perfect order and right action. Thank you, Father.

Continue your daily prayers to correct any mental cause that may have brought on the condition.

He shall call upon me, and I will answer him: I will be with him in trouble; I will deliver him, and honour him.   —Psalm 91:15

. . . WE ALL HAVE THE ABILITY TO TRANSCEND PREVIOUS EXPERIENCES . . . BUT WE SHALL NEVER TRIUMPH OVER THEM WHILE WE PERSIST IN GOING THROUGH THE OLD MENTAL REACTIONS.
                              —*The Science of Mind,* page 147

PROBLEMS OF EYESIGHT

Abnormal conditions of the eyes are treated mentally as any physical disease is. For cataracts, know that in Divine Mind there is always a clarity of vision, and that whatever seems to veil your vision of God's world is eliminated. For problems of vision as such, one would treat like this:

I know that perfect seeing is a function of the Divine Mind within me, and my healing comes as the result of my singleness of attention to the spiritual Perfection surrounding me. Thank you, God, for your wonderful world about me, and for the vision to see it.

The restoring of proper vision can be a perfectly normal result of a mental conviction based on the Wholeness of Life and Its perfect functioning at every point. Age has nothing to do with the eternal and changeless nature of God's Life within us, and there is no spiritual reason for poor eyesight! There are many physical eye problems, and a competent eye specialist can diagnose them and often render assistance. However, for one seeking a spiritual healing, it is the Divine pattern that must be proclaimed, accepted, and permitted to function. Say:

I do now accept that God's Life in me is perfect in every way. Each part of my body is some form, phase, or function of Divine Mind. I accept perfect sight, letting go of any negative idea and any subconscious resistance which would impede my clarity of vision. Right now, complete healing of my eyesight begins. Thank you, God, that it is so!

I have heard of thee by the hearing of the ear: but now mine eye seeth thee. —Job 42:5

THE MAN WHO CLEARLY REALIZES HIS ONENESS WITH ALL GOOD SHOULD HAVE STRONG, CLEAR EYESIGHT!
—*The Science of Mind,* page 230

ARTHRITIS

We believe that behind all physical ills is a kind of mental chemistry, and that thoughts are things and produce after their kind. Medical science today also teaches a mind-body relationship. A treatment to remove the mental cause of such a problem as arthritis might be as follows:

Divine Love contains no doubt, fear, resentment, or bitterness; no emotional disturbance arises within It. I place myself under Its government and let It express in my life. Where I have erred in my thoughts, emotions, and acts of personal living, I am now accepting Divine guidance so as to be healed and made new. I let my thoughts be of justice and love for all, with malice toward no one. I have absolute nonresistance to the Divine nature in human life.

It is believed that arthritis is apt to stem from mental and emotional resistance of one kind or another, usually involving relationships. So be sure to be quite honest with yourself in this respect. Continue:

I let go, right now, all need to "justify" my problems, my reactions to life, or to people. I would rather be healed than justified! I accept health and it is mine as I now give myself wholly to love—love for all. I embody this wonderful word "love" until it becomes the only power in my life.

For as the Father hath life in himself; so hath he given to the Son to have life in himself. —John 5:26

"BLESS AND CURSE NOT." . . . EVIL LASTS BUT FOR A DAY, WHILE GOODNESS SHINES TO ETERNITY AND LOVING KINDNESS IS THE VERY NATURE OF DEITY. —*The Science of Mind,* page 487

PRAYING FOR WORLD PEACE

Because of the conditions confronting man today we need to pray for peace for all people. But our prayer is to invoke within our own mind and heart a realization of God's Presence in mankind everywhere. We must identify ourselves, as well as those in high places, with that Wisdom and Love which alone can bring peace where confusion appears, healing where wrongness is, and good-will where fear and distrust abide. Let our prayer add to the light of faith which blankets the globe, that it may help dissolve the flames of hate, forestall explosions of greed, and quiet the restlessness in human hearts. Let us affirm:

Peace, like Love, is the Power at the heart of God, and God is everywhere equally present. Peace is already established within man and this word affirms that there is increased recognition and acceptance of It. Peace is a law of Life; there is no higher law, and it now finds expression in the hearts and minds of men and women in high places as well as all others in every land. The Divine destiny of this globe does not and cannot include destruction, waste, and war. The destiny of men is freedom, peace, and an abiding together so that they may unfold toward their innate Godhood. I release this word in the conviction that it adds to the forces of Good throughout this world. So let it be.

I am Alpha and Omega, the beginning and the end, the first and the last.　　　　　　　　　　　　　　—Revelation 22:13

THE GREAT LOVE WHICH I NOW FEEL FOR THE WORLD IS THE LOVE OF GOD, AND IT IS FELT BY ALL AND COMES BACK TO ME FROM ALL.
　　　　　　　　　　　　　—*The Science of Mind*, page 299

SECTION THREE

Using the Science of Mind for Answering Questions
Most Often Asked in Spiritual Counseling Situations

INTRODUCTION—III

"Doctor, I have this problem. . . ."

And whether the doctor is one of medicine, psychology, divinity, or metaphysics, here is a soul seeking help in a time of need, and there is no more important human situation than that where one person places trust in another for the healing of pain, confusion, heartache, anxiety, or any other unhappiness.

This third section is based on questions which typically emerge from such real-life situations. Each page begins with a specific inquiry that is frequently made, with the lesson (in light type) giving a suggested answer, and the personal application (in bold type) providing an example of how to treat the situation in the manner of Science of Mind.

Somewhere in these pages, you are certain to find questions you would have asked!

And indeed, you ought to ask them, for many problems persist only because the right questions were never asked. The answers are certainly there, somewhere. Nobody has yet dreamed up a human problem to which there is no answer, though sometimes the belief that "there is no way out" makes a person blind to answers and becomes an actual part of the original problem. But all illness is unnatural, all neurosis unnecessary; all grief can find consolation, all loss a compensation; and the scripture says that we should pray for one another that we may be healed!

Now, as we move into our third set of lessons, let us review the steps in the speaking of a spiritual mind treatment (there are actually many methods, with various teachers giving them different names, but the following *themes* are basic, no matter what system is followed):

GOD—Affirm your belief in God, a Power greater than you are, and keep talking until you convince yourself that God is real, is all Perfection, Life, Love, Health, Abundance.

YOURSELF—Personalize your belief in God. Know that *your* life is Divinely created and sustained; that the life within you is God-Life; that the word you now speak releases the creative Power of God, for good.

PURPOSE—State the purpose for your treatment. Name the person, situation, or condition you are treating. Name the good you desire. (This is all-important, for you must give your word specific direction.)

DENIAL—Deny that anything in yourself or others can impede or neutralize the word you now speak. Deny the necessity that any negative thing should continue. Know that there is no power stronger than God-Power.

AFFIRMATION—State clearly all of the good and perfection you can conceive about the person, situation, or condition you are treating. Know that the problem disappears *right now* as you accept the Perfection and Right Action of God.

RELEASE—Give thanks, and state that as you now release your word, you know in joy and gratitude that it is established, it is the law unto that to which it was directed.

AND SO IT IS! SO LET IT BE! AMEN!

You may wonder, "Is this, after all, nothing more than mere autosuggestion?" But even if your belief is that you are speaking only to your subconscious, it should be clear by now that whatever is the "Inner Something" to which you address yourself, the message *does* get through and something *does* happen! And so treatment may be autosuggestion, but that is not all it is, for the Power involved is greater than the self. When you turn on the lights in your house, autosuggestion may move your hand to the switch, but you do not pretend that you generated the power yourself! It came from great dynamos, perhaps thousands of miles away.

Think about that!

There is a power within *you*—greater than you, for it is the same Power that upholds the world. Yet because this Power is *your own life,* you can use It, direct It, control It, and point Its activity as you choose.

Indeed, whether you know it or not, you use this Power daily, for good or for not-so-good . . . you can't help it. Every time you believe something, each time you declare something you believe, you set into motion Universal Law, the Intelligence that is the Soul of the Universe. Fantastic? Yes, but true—and supported by the evidence of everyone who has ever tested it to determine its truth!

To "heal" your life, do not agree with problems. Reject them, and make suggestions to yourself in terms of *answers,* the positive good which reason and intuition tell you is what *ought* to be. In doing this, you are truly "calling upon the Lord," for the Lord is the Life within you—and of course much more. Yet, as the great mystic, Emma Curtis Hopkins, said, "The innermost God and the uttermost God is one God!" Know then and proclaim it again and again: THERE IS GOOD FOR ME, AND I OUGHT TO HAVE IT. IT COMES TO ME NOW ALONG PATHS OF DIVINE RIGHT ACTION.

And so it will be, for so it *is*!

A LOVED ONE'S FAITH

"What can I do to increase my son's faith in God?"

Faith is an attitude that can be developed, and we can most certainly pray to see it unfold in another person as a spiritual conviction. Every man is an expression of God, bearing the Life and Mind of the Infinite, and in each heart are the same intuitions, dreams, and needs. Yet Something within each of us seeks to express Itself through them in a unique and powerful way.

Your own belief in the omnipresence of Divine Wisdom and Its guidance must be steadfast. While you cannot learn the lessons of life for your son, you can know that in a right way for him he is guided to have an increased faith in God for the expression of his own potential. Each person lives at the level of his own understanding, but there is no limit to the spiritual insight which can daily enlarge that understanding. Remember, too, that a person's faith in God is not contingent upon his embracing any particular church doctrine. Such an association could, of course, strengthen his faith; but, essentially, it is an individual matter—a communion with and reliance upon the Divine Power, and that can happen anywhere!

So use these ideas in your prayer-treatment:

I speak this word in the belief that this one I love is a whole, complete, and perfect Son of God; that he is possessed of understanding and insight by virtue of the Spirit that is his life. This Spirit knows how to bring him into a recognition of the nature of God which indwells him. I know that as I, myself, recognize God in him, he responds to this recognition and sees for himself, and in his own way, that God is a real and present Power in his affairs.

———————

. . . Believe in the Lord your God, so shall ye be established. . . .
—II Chronicles 20:20

Faith is centered in, and co-operates with, Divine Mind.
—*The Science of Mind,* page 162

65

IMPROVING MEMORY

"Can I improve my memory?"

This is rather a common question, and its importance depends on the kind of thing that is forgotten. If you remember enough to know that you keep forgetting things, it could be not your mind but your *peace of mind* that is involved! If a man has driven a certain car for two years and suddenly forgets how to start it, the chances are that, subconsciously, there is some place he doesn't want to go!

Our subconscious is our storehouse of the knowledge placed there by our thoughts and emotions and experiences. But often we seek to block the memory of an unhappy experience, rather than healing the situation through understanding and forgiveness. When we forget a friend's telephone number, we should examine our friendship, perhaps, rather than our memory! However, there is such a thing as a memory lapse, or a series of memory lapses, which might indicate that a physical factor is involved, for the body and mind work together. No layman could properly evaluate this condition.

So let your treatment be for guidance and for reassurance:

I know that deep within my life is a center of Divinity that is untroubled, unclouded, and undisturbed. I willingly enter Its atmosphere of Peace and Wholeness now by deliberately surrendering the fears, doubts, misgivings, and resentments that block my well-being and happiness, and sincerely forgiving the mistakes of others as I would have them forgive mine. Under the guidance of Divine Intelligence I take every step necessary for perfect mental activity.

Let this mind be in you, which was also in Christ Jesus.

—Philippians 2:5

. . . MEMORY OF ITSELF IS AN UNCONSCIOUS OPERATION OF WHAT WAS ONCE A CONSCIOUS THOUGHT. —*The Science of Mind,* page 74

THE PURPOSE OF LIFE

"What is the real purpose of life?"

The best answer is probably: self-discovery. This is another way of stating the age-old maxim, "Know thyself," attributed to one of the wise men of ancient Greece and inscribed on the Temple of Apollo at Delphi. Its wisdom is eternally valid.

The foundation of our own philosophy rests upon the principle: There is One Life, that Life is God, that Life is Perfect, *and that Life is man's life.* The real self of man is the Spirit of God within him. *To know* this self is to know wisdom and harmony and wholeness and every other attribute of good, because they come from no other source—to know this is our real purpose! We believe that man is the Son of God, bearing the Divine nature of creative expression. He has the ability to know, to be consciously aware, to choose and direct his activities. When we learn to take our image of thought from the Spirit within, we shall escape the bonds of our own ignorance and enter into a more perfect expression of life.

Take time every day to be quiet and know your real self, perhaps in this manner:

I know that my life embodies the Wisdom and Love and Law of God, for my life is some part of His infinite Life. I let my thinking reflect the Divine Wholeness in which there is no confusion or lack or fear. My real self is the living Spirit, all-wise and forever perfect, making clear my way and harmonizing every situation. I completely accept this truth of my being and let it manifest.

. . . with all thy getting get understanding. —Proverbs 4:7

THE REAL SELF IS GOD AND AS SUCH IS TO BE IMPLICITLY TRUSTED. THE SPARK WHICH BURNS AT THE CENTER OF OUR OWN SOUL IS CAUGHT FROM THE LIVING AND ETERNAL FLAME OF THE SPIRIT.
—*The Science of Mind,* page 414

BAD DREAMS

"Can I stop having bad dreams?"

Let us consider this problem in relation to the principle that *all* thought is creative, but realize that not *every* thought we think is in agreement with the Truth, or the nature of God indwelling us. The dream world is the world of our unexpressed thoughts, and it is we, ourselves, who often populate this realm with wrong ideas and thoughts we have nurtured! Then we are plagued in our dreams with these phantoms of negation. Someone has said: "*You* are everything in your dream!"

Our first step toward healing this problem is to realize that we cannot avoid being exposed to unpleasantness in this world, but we need neither react to it emotionally, nor make it a part of our mental household. Since we build our whole experience on the ideas we accept with emotion and conviction, we should be *constantly discriminating* and give our attention only to those ideas which attest to the Perfection of God in us.

Instead of accepting and then repressing a negative idea, let us take a good look at it in the first place, make our decision and say "No." As we acquire this honest and straightforward habit, we will know greater self-assurance; for we will be in charge of our own thoughts, memories, and dreams, and our mental household will be cleansed!

Take the first step now and say:

I know that by choosing to accept and express ideas of good, my life will reflect the qualities of God. I choose thoughts of joy, peace, harmony, health, abundance, and success. I am filled with peace at all times; waking or sleeping, I experience only the good. And so it is.

. . . neither hearken to your dreams which ye cause to be dreamed.
—Jeremiah 29:8

TREATMENT STRAIGHTENS OUT CONSCIOUSNESS BY CLEAR THINKING.
—*The Science of Mind*, page 236

MENTAL STABILITY

"How can I help my daughter who has just been released from a mental hospital?"

We can know that the Spirit of God indwelling each person is not subject to impairment, though we often misunderstand Its nature, which results in problems of one kind or another. In spiritual mind treatment, we turn from the problem to that inner Spirit, the Presence of Wholeness and Wisdom and Love which we believe to be man's real nature, and align our thought with It. We say that this nature is the reality of man and that as we consciously identify ourselves with it we are set free from the experiences our ignorance has created. We can accept this truth about this person and know there is a response to our belief, because every thought is acted upon by the Law of Mind to manifest it.

Know this for the person you desire to help:

Divine Intelligence flows in unlimited measure through my loved one right now, giving her complete poise and self-assurance as she takes her place in society with absolute peace of mind. She is free from any fear, unrest, or problem of adjustment. God is her life, and all is well. His Love is her garment of Light, and she walks protected day and night. She sleeps in peace, wakes with gladness, and lives in perfect health! I know there is no imperfection in Spirit, and her life is spiritual, not material. She resumes her activities in joy and henceforth experiences the well-being that is her Divine heritage.

He restoreth my soul: he leadeth me in the paths of righteousness for his name's sake. —Psalm 23:3

HEALING AND DEMONSTRATION TAKE PLACE AS OUR MINDS BECOME ATTUNED TO THE TRUTH OF BEING.

—*The Science of Mind,* page 57

IMMORTALITY

"What attitude should one have about death?"

We must begin with the realization that the body is a vehicle or an instrument through which Life expresses in us on this earth plane. To accept the fact that the physical body must inevitably cease its function as the house of the Spirit does not mean that our *life* dies. It in no way contradicts our belief in eternal Life.

You are you and will go on being you when your spirit slips from the physical form in what we call "death." You need fear this no more than you fear going to sleep this evening. You would not pray to never sleep, because sleep is a law of life in the body-temple. Your transition into another dimension of living is also a law, and to be fearful of it or to pray that it never happen would be unrealistic. However, it is both realistic and right to pray or treat for complete peace of mind, and to realize that you will not pass on until your purpose here is finished and your own spirit is ready to go on. As you trust God's guidance of your life in *this* world, know that the same Presence and Power will be with you eternally, preparing your way in Love and Wisdom.

In this consciousness say:

All fear of death is now released from my mind, for I believe that I am the Son (Daughter) of the living God, and cannot cease to be. I know that God is the Author of my life, and that I am secure in Him. I spend every day of my life in expectancy of increasing good. I accept peace of mind today and always, and release all fear! "For thine is the kingdom, and the power, and the glory, for ever. Amen."

He will swallow up death in victory. . . . Isaiah 25:8

THE HIGHEST GOD AND THE INNERMOST GOD IS ONE AND THE SAME GOD. AND SO WE PREPARE NOT TO DIE, BUT TO LIVE.
—*The Science of Mind,* page 388

DISRUPTED RELATIONSHIP

"What can I do to heal a relationship disrupted through misunderstanding?"

Genuine forgiveness of the others and of oneself, regardless of what happened to cause the trouble, is the first step toward healing any misunderstanding. Pride and arrogance often keep us from expressing the courtesy we owe our fellowmen in all contacts, but they must be relinquished if the problem is to be resolved.

Faith in God's right action is the principle of healing, the secret of peace of mind. God's Spirit indwells all people; It is in you, and in the others concerned in this situation also. Give the whole matter over to Him and accept that each of you is being governed and directed by His Wisdom in such a way that all confusion is eliminated and that every effect of it is erased from your lives. To keep rehearsing the factors that caused the misunderstanding could only mean that you are not quite ready to be healed of it. The problem stays with you until at last, if only through sheer weariness, you get the humility to let God take over, accepting His Power to lift each of you into that freedom from guilt and burden and unhappiness which Wisdom and Love know how to do, and then "it will be as though it had never been."

Begin to treat or pray in this manner:

Thank you, God, for I am ready to be healed! Take my thoughts, my memories, my concerns, and heal them with Your Love—the Love which is also the healing Light in the others involved. I accept this restoration to the peace, harmony, and understanding we once knew. So let it be.

He healeth the broken in heart, and bindeth up their wounds.
—Psalm 147:3

WE ARE TOLD THAT GOD WILL FORGIVE US *after* WE HAVE FORGIVEN OTHERS. —*The Science of Mind,* page 431

71

DISCARDING GRIEF

"How do I find relief from my sorrow?"

Not to grieve for someone we love who has passed from this world would be very strange. How wonderful that we have the heart to love! But we also have the power to reason, and to surmount the feeling of loss and loneliness. Our love will suffer no loss if we do this, for real love is strengthened by true understanding. But prolonged grief is as unnatural as no grief at all. You should ask yourself what you grieve for. Do you just want your loved one with you again? All the tears in your heart will not bring him back. You know this. But if you would dry the tears, your heart could get back to the good love it knew, the happy love. How proud he would be, if you would try! When you are willing to let the grief go, the loved one comes alive again in your heart, your thoughts. His spirit was not entombed, for it is eternal Life. Nor should you shroud yours in a mantle of excessive grief, for then it becomes self-pity. Let the Spirit of God lift you! Raise Him in your heart, and He will lift you up and renew you with courage and strength.

Try using this treatment for your healing:

Thank You, God, for the reassurance in my heart right now that You are Life eternal, and my own life as well as my beloved's. Within my heart is the Love that heals and restores me to normal living. I let my grief go that joy may return, for this is the way of truth. I am now restored to happy thoughts of my loved one. I am healed now! I accept it! This word of Life brings renewed peace and faith. Thank You, Father.

. . . the Lord shall be thine everlasting light, and the days of thy mourning shall be ended.   —Isaiah 60:20

OUR CONTENTION IS NOT THAT DEAD MEN LIVE AGAIN, BUT THAT A LIVING MAN NEVER DIES.   —*The Science of Mind*, page 377

WAR FEAR

"How can I remain calm when world conditions are so threatening?"

People of strong faith have power, and if we are to put our power into peace, we should clearly, definitely, and faithfully affirm peace where war threatens, love where bitterness appears. There is no power opposed to God, regardless of any appearance. Man can develop material forces for destruction, but Divine Wisdom is *universal* Power and by contacting that supreme Power through prayer, you can help keep the peace. Believe only in God—disbelieve in evil! Pray often, in the form of such healing treatments as the following "Affirmative Prayer for National and International Good":

I believe in God! I believe in the Power of God and the Wisdom of God! I believe that the Power and Wisdom of God move as living Spirit in and through all creation, and that Divine Wisdom even now guides the leaders of our nation, and that people in high places in every nation on earth are subject to Divine guidance. I affirm that the Goodness of God is the ultimate Law unto man. This is Truth, and there is no law higher than Truth. Peace, understanding, freedom, and justice are established through the Goodness of God. All of God is everywhere present. The Peace of God is everywhere equally true, right now, among all peoples and nations on earth. This word that I speak now joins with the prayers of men, women, and children around the world, whatever their faith, whatever their language, and our prayers are one, even as God's Life in us all is One! One God, one brotherhood, one perfect state of peace on earth, right now established and inevitable! There is no power opposed to God!

. . . seek peace, and pursue it. —Psalm 34:14

THE LIGHT IS GREATER THAN THE DARKNESS NOR HAS THE DARKNESS ANY POWER OVER THE LIGHT. —*The Science of Mind,* page 411

EMOTIONAL BALANCE

"How can I help my husband, who is so irritable and short-tempered?"

It is possible to help your husband establish and maintain harmonious attitudes and feelings by realizing the truth of the situation. A sense of frustration and inadequacy is probably the main factor in his present disposition. Divine ideas stand behind everyone's thought seeking to express in every avenue of living; ideas that can place us in the right work or that can help us accomplish more satisfactorily the work we have chosen; ideas that can fulfill in a perfect way those urges for right self-expression we all have. Since your husband's life is established in God, he is centered in an Intelligence that knows how to perfect every situation that confronts him. It isn't easy to keep your own emotional balance in an atmosphere of friction, but as you do so in patience and understanding, offering no argument whatever the provocation, you will help him to be healed. Acknowledge only God's action in and through him.

Accept this truth about him:

His life is of God and he is heir to all that is ennobling and good. The ideas he is seeking to express are clearly made known to him as is the right way to use them. I affirm that even now the Divine Spirit in this man is healing his personality defect and leads him into peace of mind and a realization of the meaning of life and of the human relationships that living involves. He is now enabled by God's Love for him and in him to express lovingly, and to begin finding fulfillment through his right and natural self-expression. I accept this healing for him.

For the fruit of the Spirit is in all goodness and righteousness and truth. —Ephesians 5:9

WHEN THE INNER CONSCIOUSNESS AGREES WITH THE TRUTH . . . A DEMONSTRATION TAKES PLACE. —*The Science of Mind,* page 236

OVERWEIGHT

"Is there a solution for a weight problem?"

We should probably rather say that you have a *personality* problem! Unless there is clear medical evidence of glandular or other physical cause, the obesity is there by invitation. "You asked for it!" But just to say, "Stop eating so much" does not bring a simple cure. Yet, if obesity persists, you are either eating too much, too often, or eating unwisely; or, you are demonstrating a problem of frustration in terms of body. While this condition may be helped by more sensible habits of eating and proper exercise, it is often important to clear one's thinking of the wrong beliefs that are causing the problem. This can be done by prayer or treatment work along these lines:

I speak this word for myself, for the healing of whatever mental or physical cause there may be behind this condition of overweight. There can be no such cause in Divine Truth, which is the reality of my life. There is neither underaction nor over-action in Spirit, only right action; and I accept the discipline that accompanies it. Every cell of my body is God-Substance, and the metabolism of my body is the perfect reflection of the Divine idea of Wholeness. I am made in the image and likeness of God, whole, complete, and perfect. I now receive healing of any personality trait of sensitivity, rejection, insecurity, or any other thing that may be the hidden cause of my overweight. My mind and heart are now open to Divine guidance and to the spiritual healing of my attitudes and my emotions. Thank You, Father, for the perfection and order that now manifest through my physical being.

. . . put on the new man, which after God is created in righteous-ness. . . . —Ephesians 4:24

A NORMALLY-MINDED PERSON WILL EAT NORMALLY.
—*The Science of Mind,* page 253

INTERNAL HARMONY

"Why do I keep having intestinal trouble?"

Sometimes you can date the problem from a special incident in your past life that still troubles you. Or perhaps the circumstances are present in your life now. Strain? Tension? Economic fear? Fear of loss of prestige, person, place or thing? Or do you have a personality which is outwardly calm, but inwardly all churned up? Do you bless your food before eating? Do you bless the people about you? Were you overdisciplined as a child? Or is there someone who keeps you under too much pressure now? Above all, do you know what peace of mind is, and do you experience it often? Somewhere in the answers to these questions we might trace the mental reason or reasons for your problem. In any case a readjustment in your own thinking is basic to the healing principle. So, use this healing treatment, knowing that you will be guided into the understanding of what you must do to cooperate with the treatment, and that you accept your healing now:

Thank You, God, for the wisdom to know that there is no area in my life where Your Power does not reach—for You are my life! I realize that my body's organs and their functions are Divine ideas in form; God-Substance, perfect in principle, perfect in manifestation! The intestinal tract, the digestive system, the eliminative process, all are perfect parts of a perfectly functioning whole. My body is the temple of the indwelling Spirit, in which no disorder exists. I cease harboring ideas opposed to my Divine nature and accept my healing.

. . . and thine health shall spring forth speedily. . . .   —Isaiah 58:8

INFINITE INTELLIGENCE WITHIN ME RULES ME, AND CONTROLS AND DIRECTS ALL OF THE ORGANS OF MY BODY, SO THAT THEY FUNCTION PERFECTLY. . . .   —*The Science of Mind,* page 232

LEARNING A LANGUAGE

"Is it possible for me to learn to speak Spanish within six months?"

Nothing is better for the unfoldment of our potentials than learning something constructive! The part that mental treatment plays in any endeavor is that of a "transformer." Through prayer or treatment—turning to God, the Source of all our power—we augment, or "step up" our natural power to learn. This treatment should be helpful:

I know that my innate intelligence, which is of God, is sufficient for me to learn anything I set my attention to. I cooperate with teacher and textbook in this new study, grasping the ideas with ease and facility. I work in peace, feeling no pressure of time. I persist in this endeavor that I may rightly accomplish my desire. In this pursuit of learning I am never apart from the spiritual Power within me, guiding and inspiring me. Through this study I find new enjoyment.

You should treat for yourself in words of confidence and faith, affirming your gratitude for God's help, and for the opportunities that are opened to you as a result of this or any new study. Here is another illustration of a treatment you could use:

I am a center of Divine Intelligence, and I am aided and inspired by that Intelligence in my studies. In God's Wisdom all things are known and that Wisdom in me is my understanding of, and my ability to master, any new subject.

Whoso loveth instruction loveth knowledge. . . .   —Proverbs 12:1

WE SHOULD EXPAND OUR THOUGHT UNTIL IT REALIZES ALL GOOD, AND THEN CUT RIGHT THROUGH ALL THAT *appears* TO BE, AND USE THIS ALMIGHTY POWER FOR DEFINITE PURPOSES.

—*The Science of Mind,* page 148

ATTRACTIVENESS

"How does one become more attractive?"

We believe that the real nature of man is God's image and likeness in him, and this is the source of every attribute which is part of attractiveness. In spiritual mind treatment we identify ourselves with this inner image. The only way anyone can become more attractive is to express more of the Divine qualities. Think about your personal philosophy of life, your viewpoint on people, places, and things. Emulate only those spiritual qualities which develop in you a sound, self-confident personality. Do not try to classify yourself in worldly terms, but learn to see God wherever you are and as what you are. You should daily treat along these lines:

I believe that I am created in the image and likeness of God, and am whole, complete, and perfect. God in me is Love and Strength and Beauty. Every cell of my body shows forth the Divine laws of harmony, health, and loveliness. I accept this truth of my being and release any sense of inadequacy. The Divine image in me is superior to any past negative beliefs I have had about myself. I am conscious of God as my life—my mind, my body, and my appearance.

Do this type of treatment work consistently and with faith over a period of time, and the day will come when your friends will wonder what has happened to make you so much more attractive in appearance, so poised and self-confident.

Cast not away therefore your confidence, which hath great recompence of reward. —Hebrews 10:35

EACH HAS WITHIN HIMSELF THIS GUIDE TO TRUTH, TO REASON, TO BEAUTY. . . . —*The Science of Mind,* page 561

A CHANGE OF JOBS

"I need guidance on a possible job change."

We can trust the Cosmic purpose that impels us into new ventures since it was for some Cosmic reason that we came forth as ourselves in this world. We can best attain inner security, the key to right demonstration in our life's work, by remembering that Something greater than we are indwells our being, and seeks expression through us.

Having thought carefully about our employment, both present and prospective, considering the various factors involved, and trying to judge the good and bad points, we should accept that right action is taking place in our business affairs, and that we are clearly guided by indwelling Wisdom in our decisions.

Say to yourself:

I am rightly employed in my Father's business. I welcome change, but am willing to finish the job I have. I know that Divine Intelligence guides me to know when a job is done and when I should begin a new one. I have complete peace of mind and a sense of security with regard to my financial income, my job itself, and my ability to improve myself year by year as my life unfolds. I believe that God's will is served in the affairs of man. I am in my right place always, and if this means a change in actual employment then this will be accomplished under the right circumstances and at the right time. I know there is a right and wonderful work for me and I let no thoughts of doubt or of limitation hinder my being led to it. I express the Good wherever I am, and accept the Good which is returned to me.

In all thy ways acknowledge him, and he shall direct thy paths.
—Proverbs 3:6

GOD IS FOREVER DOING NEW THINGS, AND WHEN WE CONCEIVE NEW IDEAS, IT IS AN ACT OF THE DIVINE PROJECTING ITSELF INTO CREATION. —*The Science of Mind,* page 273

ADOLESCENCE

"How can my teenage son and I cease growing apart?"

Perhaps you are not really growing apart, it is just that the boy is growing up, and has to get through a very delicate phase of that process in terms of his own personality. He has more need than ever for the "security" he still unconsciously gets from you, simply because you are there. But he senses his isolation from the adult world. And he is right! He does not yet think as adults think. Yet his mind has developed beyond that of his childhood, where your relationship was more of an emotional oneness. His natural mental world now is that of his fellow adolescents. They are apt to be the only people he can talk to, and the only ones he believes can understand him. This is perfectly normal! But, this is the time he needs you most—don't let him down! Be aware of his development, his pursuits, his friends, but don't interfere, unless some real mistakes seem to be coming up. Be genuinely interested in him, but avoid the constant criticism which is so tempting. Let your own faith in God enter the atmosphere of your home. Realize that His nature indwells your son, too, at every stage of his life, and that Divine Intelligence knows how to fulfill each phase of his growth in a right way.

You should treat along these lines:

I am grateful for every phase of my son's unfoldment, and I greet the Divine Presence in him. I know that God's Life is this boy's life, and that infinite Wisdom teaches, befriends, empowers, and protects him. I am grateful for the joy and privilege of having this wonderful young life to care for.

And all thy children shall be taught of the Lord. . . .   Isaiah 54:13

GOD, OR SPIRIT, IS SUPREME, INFINITE, LIMITLESS PERSONALITY.
—*The Science of Mind,* page 362

BUSINESS GROWTH

"My business is about to fail; what can I do about it?"

Begin to realize that it is God you work for, and God knows nothing of failure; that an infinite Wisdom is at hand for your counsel and guidance. Then two things will happen: Your business will get back on its feet like a miracle, and you will have peace of mind such as you have never known.

Spiritual activity is not bound by precedent. No matter what the appearance of your situation may be, a constructive solution to it is available. Declare:

God is everywhere equally present, and wholly present now in this enterprise, and I accept His guidance.

The Spirit of God in man is that indwelling center of Intelligence which knows more about things than we have yet consciously realized. Every idea of good comes from this Source, but we have to be receptive—this is the very purpose of prayer. The knowledge that could save your business from this impending failure *cannot get through to you* unless you can get your conscious thought still and receptive to Truth. So you should treat for yourself like this:

I now become still, and know that God is the answer to my needs. I turn my every business problem over to God at this point, and trust His Wisdom to resolve it. I have peace of mind as I am quietly faithful to my belief in God. The guidance which I need comes at the right time and in a way I understand. I let God bring complete success into my business and into every department of my living.

The Lord will perfect that which concerneth me. . . .   —Psalm 138:8

Treatment . . . expands the consciousness and lets Reality through.   —*The Science of Mind,* page 274

SELF-HELP

"Why is it when I treat others I get results, but am unable to get results for myself?"

In the area of *self-treatment,* there is a principle of impersonality that has to be considered. It is harder to deny the reality of pain when one's own arm is aching, than it is to rise above the suggestion of pain in another person. We may have to pour forth a veritable stream of positive statements, to "get beyond the body" to a realization of Truth. Others may reach this healing conviction for us more calmly. But when we feel the problem personally, it is natural enough to have some personal fear to overcome. When our experience in treatment is frustrated, we have to get right back to fundamentals in strengthening our own belief.

For instance, you might give a good treatment for business success for someone else because you honestly believe God desires him to succeed. But when it comes to treating yourself, there may be lurking in you an old idea of limitation concerning your opportunities. If so, that's why your treatment doesn't work. Remember that in treatment you are dealing with patterns of thought, upon which the universal Law of Mind always acts impartially. This is true for all, including yourself.

Strengthen your belief with this type of treatment:

Since I know myself to be God's child, whole, complete, and perfect, I am heir to all that is good. There is no lack in Spirit and I accept Its harmonious action in this situation which concerns me. I am grateful for the right and perfect outcome.

Delight thyself also in the Lord; and he shall give thee the desires of thine heart. —Psalm 37:4

WE CANNOT DEMONSTRATE BEYOND OUR ABILITY TO MENTALLY EMBODY AN IDEA. —*The Science of Mind,* page 174

HAVING ENOUGH MONEY

"Why do I never seem to have enough money?"

Well, if you are dressed, housed, and not too hungry, then at least you have a foundation upon which to build, in gratitude. The law of increase demands a seed, and if you have anything at all it can be increased. The increase of such material good begins first in your mental and emotional life. When your viewpoint enlarges to behold greater good, then you become receptive to its influx in your life. *Prosperity is a belief, not a circumstance.* One prominent man who had gained and lost and gained again great fortunes, said he had often been broke, but never poor.

As to your particular problem—never having quite enough—let's measure it against your giving. Do you ever give enough, laugh enough, spend enough, or pray enough? Or, on the other hand, do you try to do *too* much, spend unwisely the money you *do* have?

Treat in this manner:

I know there is an absolute Principle which governs all things. I turn now from the idea of "not enough money" to the absolute certainty that I am in the midst of abundance because I am centered in God. I know that my abundance is not only something I have, but also the measure of my giving. This spiritual idea heals my lack by healing my understanding. I begin right now to enlarge my prosperity consciousness, giving and receiving in the right way and for the right reasons. I share my abundance with others, that I may continue to attract good into my life. I truly believe that it is my Father's good pleasure to give me the kingdom, and I give thanks for my abundance, and I shall use it intelligently.

The blessing of the Lord, it maketh rich, and he addeth no sorrow with it.   —Proverbs 10:22

SINCE I KNOW THE TRUTH OF MY BEING, I WILL NO LONGER HINDER OR RETARD MY GOOD FROM COMING TO ME. I WILL EXPECT AND ACCEPT ALL THAT I NEED TO MAKE LIFE HAPPY AND WORTH WHILE....
—*The Science of Mind,* page 557

MIGRAINE

"What can I do about migraine headaches?"

Often migraine patients are told by doctors that there is no specific medication for this condition when an identifiable physical cause cannot be discovered, because the condition is of a psychosomatic nature. In the Science of Mind we believe that there is no human condition outside the realm of spiritual healing, and that it is possible to heal migraine through affirmative treatment (and certainly this would be true of *psychosomatic* problems!). Divine Power is greater than the power we give to our problem. So turn to the idea that God's Life is Perfect and Harmonious, that there is no mental or physical condition which frustrates Its full expression through you. Accept your healing *now* in this treatment:

Thank You, God, for the immediate, full, and lasting healing of this problem. I know that Your Love is sufficient to bring peace of mind even as I speak these words. Whatever the cause of migraine may have been, I know that healing is now being established through the complete release of any tension or anxiety. No cause of illness exists in Spirit and it is with this center of Wholeness and Wisdom that I am unified, secure, untroubled, and at peace with the past, present, and future.

You can also treat for yourself in this manner:

I have absolute peace of mind. I release all tension, I am relaxed, and at ease always and in all ways. I forgive and accept forgiveness, and experience only the good, which is of God.

Great peace have they which love thy law: and nothing shall offend them. —Psalm 119:165

A TREATMENT FOR PEACE, ALONE, OFTEN BRINGS QUICK RESULTS WHEN ONE IS SUFFERING FROM HEADACHE.

—*The Science of Mind,* page 225

ACCIDENT PRONE

"How can I prevent having repeated accidents of one kind or another?"

Psychologists have identified a type of personality which they call "accident prone," and there are psychological tests to identify this problem. You might find it profitable to familiarize yourself with these findings. Any way which helps us understand ourselves better can contribute to our healing.

Now, how does the Science of Mind deal with this type of problem? The accidents are caused by some wrong idea in your thought that needs healing. You may have an unconscious desire for attention; you may have a repressed desire to do injury to someone, which "backfires" as injury to yourself; you may be subconsciously punishing yourself to "get even" with someone else, or with the world in general. Or the cause may be something quite different from any of these. But cause there must be, for God did not make you "accident prone"; it is something you have developed through wrong thinking. But you can heal the situation. So, begin to accept your cure through this treatment:

I know that I am a spiritual creation, a child of God, and that God's Life expresses Itself within and around me. This Life is Perfect and is not subject to harm. It enfolds me in love and wisdom and understanding. Every idea and emotion contrary to Divine Harmony is dissolved in this consciousness of my unity with God. The realization of His Presence and Power is my protection and rightly sustains me in every activity.

And ye shall know the truth, and the truth shall make you free.
—John 8:32

MAN MUST BRING HIMSELF TO THE PLACE IN MIND WHERE THERE IS NO MISFORTUNE, NO CALAMITY, NO ACCIDENT, NO TROUBLE, NO CONFUSION. . . . HE SHOULD . . . DECLARE THE TRUTH ABOUT HIMSELF. . . . —*The Science of Mind,* page 295

UNSIGHTLY DEFECT

"How can I heal an unsightly appearance?"

If you have a physical defect, there are a number of things you can do. First, bear in mind that other people's opinions of you will reflect your own evaluation of yourself. So you must heal your own wrong "mental image" of yourself and never allow yourself to indulge in self-pity. Regardless of your physical appearance, you can express the radiance of spiritual Beauty indwelling you, and you can command high respect from others through your self-confidence, moral integrity, and sincere concern for others. Be realistic in a positive way. Take stock of your attractive qualities, your talents and abilities, and put your constructive ideas to work. You can so live in a consciousness of the inner Beauty that others will see you only in Its light. In Its environment you will attract all that is worthwhile. Your physical appearance will be instantly improved, even in a *physical* way, when you radiate such confidence and faith.

Here is a type of treatment that will be helpful:

I know that the Divine Spirit within me expresses through me in harmony, love, and peace. I let these qualities flow through me now to illumine me and make my life truly beautiful. Real beauty is soul deep; and I find joy in acting upon the constructive ideas that flow to me from the Spirit within, impelling me to express the fullness of love and friendship and success. I give thanks for my blessings and I use them to bless my world.

And let the beauty of the Lord our God be upon us. . . .
—Psalm 90:17

THE ONES TO WHOM WE ARE MOST STRONGLY ATTRACTED ARE NOT NECESSARILY THE ONES WHO ARE THE MOST BEAUTIFUL PHYSICALLY, BUT ARE THE ONES FROM WHOM WE RECEIVE THAT SUBTLE EMANATION . . . THAT WHICH EMANATES FROM WITHIN.
—*The Science of Mind,* page 296

SCHOOLWORK

"My son does poorly at school. Can treatment help him?"

There is a right mental treatment for every human problem, because spiritual mind treatment involves spiritual faith, and the God we have faith in can heal anything! In treating for your boy, the first thing to do is to remember that his life is God, and is perfect, complete and whole. This perfection is not yet fully revealed, even in you or me, but it is the essence of our being, and our inescapable ultimate demonstration. Just as with a plant there is the shoot, the bud, the flower, and the fruit; so, in the case of young people, the unfoldment is also very definitely going to progress through what we call "stages of growth."

You should treat for your boy in this manner:

I recognize and bless God's wonderful Life in my son, and I know that Divine Mind is unfolding within and through him, and is expressing Its Wisdom in terms of his own growing understanding. For this I am grateful!

In handling the actual school problem, here again treatment is the answer. Treat something like this:

The Spirit of Life within my son, the God of his being, is even now at work within him causing him to be interested, alert, and intelligently motivated. My son is a working part of the school he attends, in harmony with his teachers, his studies, and his fellow students. He is well-balanced, and happy in his studies. He works well at the level of his understanding, which daily increases. I am grateful for God's unceasing guidance, and I release this word in faith. So let it be.

So teach us to number our days, that we may apply our hearts unto wisdom.
—Psalm 90:12

REMEMBER THAT THE THOUGHT OF THE PARENTS INFLUENCES THE CHILD.
—*The Science of Mind*, page 210

PERSONALITY CLASH

"What attitude should I take toward someone who seems to dislike me?"

Every once in a while you meet someone who feels antagonistic toward you for no apparent reason. Perhaps consciously or unconsciously this person is associating you with someone he felt did him an injustice at one time or another. But a healing atmosphere can be brought into your necessary dealings with him if you view him from the spiritual level rather than from the personal. The Spirit in man knows no antipathy, is never resentful or angry.

Even though this person may not believe in God the way you do, and because of environment and the habits of personal thinking there may have been built up a rather unpleasant personality, still there exist within him the high qualities with which God has endowed us all. Identify this person in your own mind with these qualities at all times. This is what prayer is— seeing God where the trouble seems to be. So when you pass nearby this person, say mentally, "The God in me salutes the God in you."

You can establish a new air of peace and friendly responsiveness by using affirmative thoughts or statements such as these:

The Spirit of God in me salutes that same Spirit in him. I withdraw all resistance to the Life of God in this man. I have peace of mind and the expectancy of only good relations.

When we know this truth, we must use it for ourselves and for others until they, too, learn the way of God. We must keep our own consciousness clear by knowing that God is the only Person, the only Power, right here, right now.

If we live in the Spirit, let us also walk in the Spirit.

—Galatians 5:25

THOUGHT CAN ATTRACT TO US THAT WHICH WE FIRST MENTALLY EMBODY. . . .   —*The Science of Mind,* page 294

FINDING HAPPINESS

"How can I find happiness?"

The search for happiness, in itself, is apt to prove futile and disillusioning, for happiness is not an object that can be found and grasped, it is a quality of heart—a by-product of the life that is God-centered and fully expressing the Divine qualities.

Unhappiness is unnatural, and prolonged unhappiness indicates a neurotic, hidden need to cling to it for some reason. Loneliness is usually self-imposed. You cannot be happy or know the rewards of living if you separate yourself from the life-stream of social cooperation. Love, joy and harmony are universal qualities, and will become the fabric of your own life when you are continually centered in the Good and associated with those who are expressing God.

Use this treatment to enlarge your consciousness:

I know that happiness now permeates my life, as the sunshine permeates the atmosphere, for I am established in Spirit. I know that my joy is not dependent on any special person, place, or thing, but results from my constant recognition and acceptance of the Divine Good expressing through all life, everywhere. I now accept joy in my relationships and harmony in my affairs and activities. I have a Divine companionship with all people. I am grateful for the rich gifts of Life and I seek ways to share them with others. I am now and henceforth shall be receptive in thought and feeling to Divine Joy, that It may express in unlimited measure in my experience.

For ye shall go out with joy, and be led forth with peace. . . .
—Isaiah 55:12

HAPPINESS . . . A STATE OF INNER PEACE, A CONSCIOUSNESS OF THE GOODNESS OF GOD AND THE BENEFICENT ATTITUDE OF THE UNIVERSE, A REALIZATION THAT JOY CAN COME TO EVERY MAN.
—*The Science of Mind,* page 597

ABOUT THE AUTHOR

Craig Carter, D.D., RSc.D., is Minister of the First Church of Religious Science, Dallas, Texas. Ordained a Religious Science minister in 1950, his former pastorates include churches in California and Nevada. Author of *Your Handbook for Healing* (DeVorss & Co., Los Angeles), Dr. Carter is especially known for his innovative "healing missions." He has lectured nationwide on metaphysical healing methodologies, parapsychological research, mysticism, and comparative religion.

Prior to his ministerial career, Dr. Carter, an alumnus of the University of California at Berkeley, was with the United States Foreign Service, serving in China and Egypt, his last post being as Vice Consul and Chinese Language Secretary at Nanking.

He has contributed regularly to *Science of Mind* Magazine for twenty-five years.

For additional information about the Science of Mind or Science of Mind *Magazine, write P.O. Box 75127, Los Angeles, California 90075.*